AWAKENED BY THE SPIRIT

RECLAIMING THE FORGOTTEN GIFT OF GOD

RON M. PHILLIPS

OLIVER NELSON™

THOMAS NELSON PUBLISHERS
Nashville

Published in Nashville, Tennessee, by Thomas Nelson, Inc.

Library of Congress Cataloging-in-Publication Data

Phillips, Ron M.
 Awakened by the Spirit / reclaiming the forgotten gift of God / Ron M. Phillips
  p. c.m.
 Includes bibliographical references.
 ISBN 0-7852-6901-0 (pbk.)
  1. Baptists—Doctrines. 2. Phillips, Ron M.—Religion.
3. Pentecostalism. 4. Evangelicalism. I. Title.
 BX6331.2.P45 1999
 286'.132—dc21   99-39350
                                                              CIP

This volume is lovingly dedicated to my children,
Kevin and Kelli Phillips Logue,
and
Cain and Heather Phillips Wooten.

Your own quest for authentic Christianity has stirred my
spirit to a deeper walk. Long before me, you saw the
emptiness of church without Christ, faith without fire, and
law without love. May you be inspired to walk in the fullness
and reality of the living Christ.

Also, to Ronnie Jr., may your ministry begin in fire and
fullness as you come to know the God of miracles intimately.
And to my lovely wife, Paulette: you have made the journey
with me, and your ministry is just beginning.

CONTENTS

Contents

FOREWORD

$\mathcal{T}$his book deserves a careful reading. The temptation of many a reader will be to put it back on the shelf because it presents what to some is an alternative view of the person, ministry, and gifts of the Holy Spirit. I generally buy a book according to author. There are several questions that call for an answer before I invest time in a book.

Is the author a broken man? Real humility issues only out of brokenness. I have walked close to Ron Phillips for a good many years. Brokenness is not a one-time experience but a position of commitment. When there would have been none to fault his running from the issue, Ron stayed by the stuff and came out as pure as gold.

Does the author's walk match his message? None who really know Ron will answer with less than a resounding yes! He walks with God, hears from God, and speaks with anointing from God.

Does the message of the author resonate in a dynamic ministry? I have visited the Central Baptist Church on several occasions and witness to its increasingly dynamic vision and program. In 1998 and again in 1999 I was on the program at the Fresh Oil and New Wine Conference and had the distinct feeling that the first conference would prove to be "the shot heard around the world" in evangelical circles. Pastors in these meetings returned to their churches with fresh vision and fire. The ministry of Ron Phillips reaches far beyond the grounds of the dynamic Central Baptist Church.

Finally, I ask, has the author made the discovery of the God among us without a body, the Holy Spirit incoming, indwelling, and manifesting Himself inside him? Some readers may disagree with terminology and even emphases but none of us would succeed in downplaying the authentic ring of the contents herein. His position on "the baptisms" is challenging as he differentiates between positional, pictorial, and powerful baptism.

None will want to miss his vital chapters on the church as a new wineskin and the church of the future.

The book throbs with life and expectation and leaves the reader absolutely convinced that there is much more available than we have imagined if we dare to pursue it under the direction of the Spirit of God.

Thank you, Ron. A large segment of the body of Christ has waited for a book like this—a simple, no-ax-grinding, straightforward, in-your-face presentation. Thank you for giving a new meaning to the challenge to "go for it!" We take courage from you.

JACK TAYLOR
Dimensions Ministries
Melbourne, Florida

PREFACE

$\mathcal{A}$s I take pen in hand to write this book, there are several convictions that will guide me. First, I do not wish in any way to offend or forget my brothers and sisters in Christ with whom there may be points of disagreement. The apostle Paul advised us,

> For you, brethren, have been called to liberty; only do not use liberty as an opportunity for the flesh, but through love serve one another. For all the law is fulfilled in one word, even in this: "You shall love your neighbor as yourself." But if you bite and devour one another, beware lest you be consumed by one another! (Gal. 5:13–15 NKJV)

I fear that too often we Southern Baptists and other evangelicals are known more by what we are *against* than what we are *for*. We tend to operate in a reactive way toward others. Obviously, the great moral questions often demand negative reaction from the church. Yet this same reactive spirit is sometimes turned toward genuine brothers and sisters who embrace biblical authority yet may disagree on some interpretations.

Second, what I have learned and experienced has come not from a classroom or a study, but in the heat of battle. The graces, gifts, and manifestations of the Holy Spirit came upon me in the throes of adversity, persecution, near death experiences, and spiritual warfare.

My heart cry is, "If I must boast, I will boast in the things which concern my infirmity" (2 Cor. 11:30 NKJV).

From 1978 to 1989, I was in the middle of the Southern Baptist struggle for sound doctrine and the inerrancy of Scripture. Every year I rallied hundreds of messengers to vote for the right candidates and causes. During those years I served on many boards and committees on every level of denominational life. I served for eight years on the North American Mission Board (former Home Mission Board) and was chairman of that board in my last year of service. Make no mistake, I have loved my denomination. Yet I sensed in my spirit that something wasn't quite right. Even when the battle was over, it seemed that there had been a further narrowing of the parameters in defining who we are.

I listened as Christians in other denominations were characterized as "dangerous." There were rantings about how the charismatic crowd was certainly to be avoided and not embraced. Of course, we were using the charismatic influence, their TV networks, and their music, all the while secretly calling them demonized or emotionally unstable! We would "use" certain individuals in their camp whom we considered safe, sincerely hoping that there would be no embarrassing use of tongues or other spiritual manifestations.

I flailed away at these groups for many years, parroting the party line that all this supernatural stuff was unnecessary, tongues had ceased, falling was demonic, and trembling was emotional excess. Praise and worship could be loud and boisterous, but watch out for the hand raisers and jumpers. No one was to actually expect tangible miracles or healings anymore. The mystery of faith was reduced to formulas. I knew that if you didn't hold to these interpretations, you became persona non grata. You were out! In the name of "love" it would soon spread that you were "one of them."

And then, from the Southern Baptist LifeWay Christian Resources came *Experiencing God* by Henry Blackaby. All our adult Bible study

groups at Central Baptist Church where I pastor completed the *Experiencing God* study.[1] We began to discover what God was doing and learned to adjust our lives accordingly. We found out God was working powerfully beyond the borders of our tradition. We dared to look around, and we found the Lord graciously at work in others.

What God has wrought in our church and in other evangelical churches has happened in times of need and desperation.

Third, I wish to stand firmly on the fact that biblical principles establish for us what is possible in church worship today. Although God did not choose to give us a chapter and verse on every detail of every decision we ever make, He laid out clear principles that we should apply to our daily walk, both in the church and in our personal lives. History gives testament to the fact that when people follow biblical principles, God's power is released in mighty ways.

Some church leaders in our day lift certain doctrines and belief systems higher than the Word of God. I was guilty of doing this. I clung for years to the trend toward *cessationism*, or the belief that the sign gifts of the Holy Spirit (tongues, prophecy, healing) ceased at the close of the biblical canon. There is little support for that position in the major commentaries, church history, and Christianity as a whole. Nevertheless, a few evangelicals continue printing books and writing articles as if it were the orthodox view of conservative Christianity. The truth is—it is the minority view. I was blinded to that fact, however, and stubbornly refused to study it out for myself, perhaps because I was afraid of what I would discover.

Jesus warned us in all three of the synoptic Gospels about the "leaven of the Pharisees." Matthew's gospel reported His caution this way: "Then Jesus said to them, 'Take heed and beware of the leaven of the Pharisees and the Sadducees.' . . . Then they understood that He did not tell them to beware of the leaven of bread, but of the doctrine of the Pharisees and Sadducees" (16:6, 12 NKJV).

The Pharisees pressed the grid of their commentaries and traditions on Scripture. Soon they believed their own interpretations were equal to God's Word. The group wrote the Mishnah, a commentary on the Scriptures, and the Gemara, a commentary on commentaries, and then proclaimed that the Bible was water but the commentaries were wine. They searched the Scriptures, but missed Jesus.

In this book, I want to issue an alternate approach to those who desire to take another look at the Bible without the grid of some system and simply let it speak. Let us look honestly at the Scriptures and ask, "Where is the power of God?" Together we will take a fresh look at church history. Let us not be revisionists, rewriters of history, trying to press our own interpretations upon the past, but let us look objectively at what God did. We will read the testimonies of evangelicals still among us who have been touched by the fire of the Holy Spirit, some of whom were disenfranchised for their stand.

We will investigate the theories of people who are teaching that there were three periods of miracles. Does the Bible even teach that? What proof can be brought forth?

We will ask other questions such as these: Is there an explanation for revival manifestations such as falling, trembling, weeping, laughing, and others? Did this weird stuff happen in church history? Did it ever happen among Baptists? Does it happen today?

What about praise and worship? Is it biblical to clap? To raise your hands? To move your body? Are praise choruses and other new styles of music a passing fad?

As we examine each of these subjects, we will hear from Scripture, history, and contemporary evangelicals, and we will allow our hearts to absorb the powerful work and ministry of the Holy Spirit that continue in lives today. I pray that you will ask yourself the question that I had to face: Is the power of God real in my life?

ACKNOWLEDGMENTS

I must thank my friend and partner, Margy Barber, who labored with me to birth this book. I can never thank her enough for her creativity, research, and rewriting. This book would not have been possible without her.

I am grateful to Larry Hargrave, who challenged me to undertake this book, along with Victor, Brian, Rose Marie, Doris, and all our friends at Thomas Nelson Publishers who have encouraged me.

Special thanks to Phil Hoskins, Rick Amato, and Rick White, true brothers who have encouraged my spiritual journey with the Lord and challenged me in my writing ministry. Also, I appreciate my friend Bailey Smith, who lets me know when he disagrees with me and loves me anyway!

A big thank you to a wonderful church family and supportive staff who have shown such patience and support throughout these months of writing.

Finally, I am profoundly grateful for Fred, who challenges me to excellence; Eddie, who keeps me on time; Jim, who calms my spirit; Angie, who won't let me quit; and to Carolyn, who supports my every undertaking. Thank you!

Part 1

A FRESH START

Chapter 1

A JOURNEY OUT
OF DEATH

*A*s my plane sped westward toward my destination for a speaking engagement, I felt my life as I had known it for twenty-two years had come to an end. At age forty-two, the dew of my youth had long since dried up. *I have reached what would be considered by many to be the pinnacle of evangelical life. I serve a large and growing congregation of Christians. My family is intact and devoted. How can I feel so inadequate and miserable?* These thoughts tumbled over and over in my mind.

Fumbling with my laptop, I began to write out my resignation to the ministry. My mind reflected on the years of my life. I remembered the deep conviction of the Holy Spirit on my life at the age of eight. The fires of revival and harvest swept through Montgomery, Alabama. Our young church met in a tent for weeks. A powerful evangelist named C. E. Autrey preached at the meetings, and the fire of God fell for two weeks. I trembled and wept with conviction at every gathering of the church.

Finally, my pastor, John Bob Riddle, spoke to me in the front seat of his car on a late summer afternoon. Although I was too shy to pray in front of my pastor, after he drove away I bowed on my knees beside a swing set in my backyard and prayed for Jesus to save me. I remember flopping down onto the grass afterward, and gazing up into the stars, I felt as though I were floating right through them.

At age fourteen, I felt God tugging at my heart with a call to preach. At the time, I resisted His gentle prodding because I feared the prospect of speaking in front of others. God continued His work in my heart, however, and when I was sixteen years old, I ran down an aisle at a youth revival, yielding my life to His service. I was so overcome with emotion and tears at the altar that the minister couldn't understand my incoherent confession of my decision. When others told him later of my call to preach, the godly man wasted no time in giving me a preaching assignment in a service.

Thus, my spiritual life began with an overwhelming conversion experience and a fiery call to the ministry. It was a natural step at the age of eighteen to further my training at Clarke College, a Baptist institution, in Newton, Mississippi. There I gained a number of friends who loved to speak of spiritual things and the power of the Holy Spirit. During a school break, my friend Dr. Ken Cheek took me to Camp Zion in Myrtle, Mississippi, where I first felt the longing for more of God.

Later that year, I was invited to speak at a weekend youth revival with Bill Henderson, a pastor from Natchez, Mississippi. I failed miserably in my preaching effort on Friday evening, preaching every sermon I had in the course of twenty minutes. Early the next morning, Bill took me in a back room and asked me if I had ever been filled with the Holy Spirit. I confessed that I had not, and I didn't know what he was talking about. He laid hands on me and prayed, and I felt a surge of power rush through me. I preached with a greater anointing the rest of the weekend. I learned that preaching only with your mind and intellect was not sufficient.

I left those early experiences behind and went on to Samford University at age nineteen. While a student, I became a pastor of a small church. A year later, Paulette and I were married, and our lives were caught up in an unceasing succession of school and church activities that went on for seven years.

In 1974, I received my doctorate from New Orleans Baptist Theological Seminary. With my degree, a wife, and the addition of two precious daughters, we moved to minister in Alabama. In the next five years, I consecutively pastored two churches, seeing both ministries complete building and remodeling projects as the attendance thrived.

In 1979, I was called to pastor at Central Baptist Church in Hixson, Tennessee, where I currently serve, and the Lord continued to bless. My family soon expanded with the addition of a son. We began radio and TV ministries, broke records in church giving and attendance, and completed several new building projects.

The years of ministry brought me much success in religious life. However, I felt burned out instead of on fire for God. I knew how to play the game, draw a crowd, and stay in favor with the people who counted. Yet personally, I was miserable.

What had happened to my first love? Where had the passion to preach gone? Where was the joy of ministry?

Back on that airplane, I finished typing a one-page resignation just as we touched down in Albuquerque. I decided to complete the speaking assignment, return to my church, and quit.

Upon my arrival at the conference center, I found my room and then made my way to hear the evening speaker, Mrs. Minette Drumwright. Since my assignment to speak was not until the next morning, I sat in the back so that I could make an easy exit if the session proved to be boring. After all, in my fundamentalist world, women were not considered to have much to say.

Was I in for a surprise!

Mrs. Drumwright began to share about the tragic and untimely death of her husband, Huber, who had been a minister and denominational executive. His sudden death had brought her face-to-face with her own spiritual needs. She confessed that her husband had been her spiritual support, and at his death, she felt as though her spiritual foundation had been suddenly kicked out from under her. She announced that a fresh filling of the Holy Spirit and a new walk with the Lord had sustained her.

Such words were not new to me. I had read *The Key to Triumphant Living* by Jack Taylor.[1] I had read R. A. Torrey's testimony on the baptism of the Holy Spirit. At a previous state conference, I had heard Stephen Olford's eloquent call to the Spirit-filled life. In fact, I had across the years experienced temporary touches of the power of God.

Yet I refused to believe in a second blessing. I reasoned that the Holy Spirit stuff was for the charismatics. I was an educated pastor who could read the Greek New Testament.

Despite those thoughts, I undeniably felt all of my prejudice melt away as I tearfully left that hall for my room. I fell exhausted across my bed and slumbered into a fitful sleep.

In the night, I heard my name being called. The voice was deep and clear. Going to the door, I found no one there. I returned to my sleep, but I was certain that I had heard my name called. Before long, I heard my name called again. Startled, I got up and looked down the hall and out the window. No one seemed to be there.

As I was awakened a third time, my room was filled with God's presence. It was the voice of my dear Savior. I wept as the glory filled the room, and I cried out, "Lord, where have You been?"

He said to me, "I have been waiting for you."

I asked, "Lord, where have You been waiting?"

He replied, "Read your Scripture for today."

It was my discipline to read five psalms a day, and since it was the nineteenth day of the month, I opened my Bible to Psalm 91 and read these assuring words:

> He who dwells in the secret place of the Most High
> Shall abide under the shadow of the Almighty.
> I will say of the LORD, "He is my refuge and my fortress;
> My God, in Him I will trust." (Ps. 91:1–2 NKJV)

There was a secret place, an intimate place, where I could meet Him and receive power. I read on to discover that I could be anointed with fresh oil:

> But my horn You have exalted like a wild ox;
> I have been anointed with fresh oil. (Ps. 92:10 NKJV)

Soon His presence and anointing overcame me. Fresh oil and new wine poured into my dry and thirsty soul. It was the baptism of power. I wept, sang, laughed, shouted, shook, and lay at peace before Him. I did not receive a prayer language then—that would come three years later—but I left that place never to be the same. I had moved into a new realm of communication and power with God. A fire burned in my soul that rages until this very day. A burning passion for Jesus and a desire to do His will came upon my life.

SORE TRIALS

Within two short years of that experience, I was faced with trials in every area of my life. My wife, Paulette, was nearly killed in a terrible car crash. For more than four months she required personal care. Those were difficult months. I had to let go of a lot of my usual responsibilities so that I could properly care for my wife and family

A few months later, my dad died unexpectedly. Just as many in bereavement have come to realize, I knew there were things that I wished I could have said to him, and I was in grief that I did not get to say good-bye.

Then came the blow of all blows. One of my associate pastors in the church was arrested and revealed to be a pedophile. His sinful acts generated a storm of bad publicity for the ministry. Members as well as nonmembers called my integrity into question. Eventually, the church was sued for $10 million. It was a dark moment.

One evening in the midst of this crisis, my heart seemed to stop, and I fainted. Rushed to the hospital, I was told that I had a "heart incident." Late that evening, someone came into the room and prayed over me for my healing. My heart was found to be undamaged and God restored my health, but the close call took its toll on my hurting spirit.

My associate Reverend Gaylon Wiley suffered a heart attack and received dire warnings about the future. He recovered and continued serving God with fresh anointing. In spite of the crisis confronting our church, I watched and rejoiced to see God direct Spirit-filled men and women to join our staff, each one bringing fresh enthusiasm and specific giftings to enable the church ministry to expand.

In the meantime, I found that the crisis in the church had caused many fellow Baptist pastors across the denomination to withdraw from me. Most local pastors rushed to take advantage of our problem by encouraging our concerned members to join their churches. Outsiders warned newcomers and prospects that our church had insurmountable problems and would probably not survive.

RENEWAL IN THE CHURCH

While skeptics predicted our church would likely go to pieces, the very opposite proved to be true. The church grew at a rate of two for every one who left. Questions and discussion concerning the crisis were handled privately so that church business and worship were never hindered. The staff and deacons were trusted to take care of the problems.

Many more of our people began to move in the power of the Holy Spirit. In the midst of a staff prayer meeting in the fall of 1992, God spoke clearly that He would grow the church if we would allow Him to do a "new thing." This word was based on these verses from Isaiah:

> When you pass through the waters, I will be with you;
> And through the rivers, they shall not overflow you.
> When you walk through the fire, you shall not be burned,
> Nor shall the flame scorch you . . .
> For I will pour water on him who is thirsty,
> And floods on the dry ground;
> I will pour My Spirit on your descendants,
> And My blessing on your offspring . . .
> No weapon formed against you shall prosper. (Isa. 43:2; 44:3; 54:17 NKJV)

The power of God fell in that room, and we left there with the assurance that all would be well with the body.

THE NO-NO

In 1993 I received a prayer language while prostrate before God as I was making intercession for a fellow pastor. God spoke the interpretation to my spirit, and it concerned a possible job change by this pastor. I called to warn him not to take the job of associate at another church. He had that confirmed in his spirit. A week later the pastor who was trying to hire him left the work. If my friend had taken that job, he would have been left high and dry.

As I will explain in a later chapter, I have since learned of the great benefits involved in the gift of a spiritual language.

During that season of my life, I also learned of the reality of the demonic world. I woke up to spiritual warfare and discovered the secret to continuous victory in Christ. These truths, which I share later, would shake our church out of complacency into spiritual health.

THE RECORD STANDS

Revival as awakening broke out in our church, and wave after wave of blessing has flowed ever since. Membership, attendance, and finances have more than doubled, even though hundreds have left who were fearful of the move of God. The church's ministry is worldwide via television, radio, and printed media. Thousands are walking in fullness and freedom today.

All of the distinct signs of revival have followed, bringing the church under scrutiny and criticism. People have been saved, healed, and delivered from demons. They have trembled, wept, laughed, shouted, and fallen in the Spirit. Praise and worship, including singing, clapping, hand raising, body movement, and spiritual singing, continue to mark the services.

Are these experiences valid? Is what is happening biblically accurate? Did these signs happen in church history? The following chapters will give biblical and historical evidence for the work of God going on today. There will also be a call to the religious who do not believe in the power of the Holy Spirit. The structures of religion often have in the past been the enemy of Jesus Christ. Both the liberal Sadducees and the fundamentalist Pharisees got together to kill Jesus. Religion invariably opposes the new work of God. Read on to be challenged in your heart about the Holy Spirit.

Chapter 2

THE BAPTISM OF THE HOLY SPIRIT

The key to my whole new life was the baptism with the Holy Spirit. Others may choose another name for this experience, but I choose the biblical name. God came on me afresh and ushered me into His presence. I gained a more intimate walk with the Lord through this powerful release of God's presence on my life.

I believe that this climactic special moment is a mark on all of God's powerful servants of the past. Many speak of God's anointing as a sacred moment and the beginning of a new realm of ministry for them.

One of these mighty servants of history was R. A. Torrey. Torrey had been a Christian in the ministry for years when suddenly in the course of his Bible study, he found his attention strongly attracted to phrases in Scripture such as "filled with the Spirit," "the gift of the Holy Spirit," and "the Holy Spirit fell upon them." He wrote of his subsequent quest for the power of God in his own life:

As I studied the subject still further, I became convinced that they described an experience which I did not myself possess, and I went to work to secure for myself the experience thus described. I sought earnestly that I might be "baptized with the Holy Spirit." I went at it very ignorantly. I have often wondered if anyone ever went at it more ignorantly than I did. But while I was ignorant, I was thoroughly sincere and in earnest, and God met me, as He always meets the sincere and earnest soul, no matter how ignorant he may be. God gave me what I sought; I was baptized in the Holy Spirit. And the result was a transformed Christian life and a transformed ministry.[1]

Another man of God who refused to operate without the power of the Holy Spirit was D. L. Moody. Early in his ministry, he pushed forward in his work, operating mostly in the strength of his own flesh. He felt he had no real power in his life, but he didn't know how to resolve that problem.

At the close of his meetings in a YMCA, two humble Free Methodist women often approached him and said, "We are praying for you." Their comment unnerved the young preacher.

Finally one night on their approach, he asked, "Why are you praying for me? Why don't you pray for the unsaved?"

They responded, "We are praying that you may get the power." He asked what they meant, and they proceeded to explain to him the definite baptism of the Holy Spirit. He then prayed with the women, fervently desiring the power of God to fall on his life.

Not long after that prayer, as he was walking in the midst of the hustle and bustle of the streets of New York, the power of God fell upon Moody so mightily that he had to turn aside to the house of a friend. There, alone in a room for hours, he experienced a filling of his soul with such joy that he at last had to ask God to withhold His hand. He went out from there with the power of the Spirit upon him, and going directly to a London crusade, he saw God do a wondrous work through him, bringing hundreds into the church.[2]

I could write pages and pages of the men of God who have experienced the filling of the Spirit, such as Charles Spurgeon, Billy Sunday, Charles Finney, and Evan Roberts, the Welsh evangelist. However, God's power is not just for great preachers of the faith. It is God's desire for all Christians to know the power of the Holy Spirit upon them.

Take a look with me at the biblical material about the baptism with the Holy Spirit.

IS THERE ONE BAPTISM?

Just the mention of the baptism of the Holy Spirit causes hackles to rise on most of my contemporaries. The traditional view is that the baptism with the Holy Spirit is what Paul mentioned in 1 Corinthians 12:13 (NKJV): "For by one Spirit we were all baptized into one body—whether Jews or Greeks, whether slaves or free—and have all been made to drink into one Spirit."

Ephesians 4 is cited to make the argument for only one baptism in the believer's life. This passage refers to "one Lord, one faith, one baptism" (v. 5 NKJV). Thus, opponents of God's work conclude, "You see, all of this talk of a baptism of the Spirit following conversion is foolish." They then want to disclaim what they call a second work of grace.

In Acts 19, Paul discovered another group that had taken part in John's water baptism but were not fully informed about Jesus. He declared the truth to them, and they were baptized in the name of Jesus. It appears that in Ephesus some people were teaching two water baptisms, one to recall John the Baptist and one to be performed in obedience to Jesus. Paul taught that only one water baptism was needed, and that should take place after conversion.

Hebrews 6:2 (NKJV) speaks of "the doctrine of baptisms." Notice it is plural. At least *three* baptisms belong to every believer: positional, pictorial, and powerful.

As noted earlier, Paul stated, "For by one Spirit we were all baptized into one body" (1 Cor. 12:13 NKJV). This speaks of *positional* baptism, which takes place at the time that the Holy Spirit places a person into the church, the body of Christ. This is a once-and-for-all act whereby the Spirit unites the individual to the body of Christ.

The *pictorial* baptism is water baptism, an event that portrays the death, burial, and resurrection of Christ. There is only one water baptism as taught in Ephesians 4, and it is by immersion subsequent to salvation.

The *powerful* baptism is the baptism with the Holy Spirit given by Jesus. The triune God is involved fully in this baptism as well: it was promised by the Father, bestowed by the Son, and performed by the Holy Spirit.

What a joy to read the words spoken by John the Baptist in Luke 3:16 (NKJV): "I indeed baptize you with water; but One mightier than I is coming, whose sandal strap I am not worthy to loose. He will baptize you with the Holy Spirit and fire."

Simply stated, the baptism with the Holy Spirit and fire is the coming of power and anointing upon an individual so that he may carry out his part of God's work.

Although the believer receives the Holy Spirit at conversion, He is *released* to work in the believer's life at the baptism with the Holy Spirit. Many would say that the positional baptism of 1 Corinthians 12:13 is the same as the powerful baptism of Luke 3:16. But if it is the same, then where is the power of God on your people? Where is the evidence in their character and witness? Where is the unmistakable seal of God's fire and power? You see, it just doesn't add up.

LOOK AT JESUS

No one would deny that Jesus always had the Holy Spirit within Him. Yet at His baptism, all four Gospels agree: "He saw the Spirit of God descending . . . and alighting upon Him" (Matt. 3:16 NKJV; see also Mark 3:10; Luke 3:22); and the Spirit "remained upon Him" (John 1:32 NKJV). Jesus received an equipping and anointing with power. If Jesus received such a blessing, who are we to deny the need in our own lives?

Peter made reference to Jesus' anointing by the Holy Spirit in his sermon to the gentile Cornelius's household:

> That word you know, which was proclaimed throughout all Judea, and began from Galilee after the baptism which John preached: how God anointed Jesus of Nazareth with the Holy Spirit and with power, who went about doing good and healing all who were oppressed by the devil, for God was with Him. (Acts 10:37–38 NKJV)

The result of this teaching on Cornelius and his company was the same experience: "The Holy Spirit fell upon all those who heard the word" (Acts 10:44 NKJV). Many ask, "Couldn't someone get all of this at once?" The answer is yes. On rare occasions a person may be saved, empowered by the Spirit, and baptized in water on the same day. Most of us, however, have not had that kind of experience. Some scholars believe that the sealing of the Holy Spirit in Ephesians 1:13 is the work of spiritual enduement subsequent to conversion. D. Martyn Lloyd-Jones, the great Anglican scholar; A. J. Gordon; R. A. Torrey; and D. L. Moody are among those who believe in a special enduement of God's Holy Spirit.

THE EVIDENCE OF THE BAPTISM
WITH THE HOLY SPIRIT

Some believe that the gift of tongues is the initial evidence of the baptism of the Holy Spirit. I do not believe that is accurate. Tongues and other signs are by-products of the baptism with the Spirit. Speaking in tongues may be one evidence of God at work but certainly is not declared to be a required evidence anywhere in Scripture.

The evidence of the baptism with the Holy Spirit is power. *Dunamis* is the Greek word translated "power." It is the word for explosive, supernatural, transforming power. The believer receives this power at the baptism with the Holy Spirit.

My question is not, Do you speak with tongues? but, Is the power of God on your life? If His power is on your life, then the ministry of Jesus becomes your ministry.

THE ANOINTING OF THE HOLY SPIRIT

The power released by the Holy Spirit enables the believer to do good and to set the oppressed free. Is your life so full of power that those chained by the devil can be set free and saved through your influence? Have you received this anointing, this sealing, and this baptism?

HUNG UP ON WORDS

Perhaps you feel uncomfortable or want to argue about the nomenclature or terminology used as you read this chapter. Listen, whether you call it a hot dog, a Coney, a wiener, a weenie, a sausage, or a frankfurter, it still tastes the same when you put the mustard on it. The issue is, Have you received an outpouring of

God's power on your life? If not, why not? Stop quibbling over terminology, and begin to claim your fullness now.

How Can I Be Baptized with the Holy Spirit?

To be baptized with the Holy Spirit, take these steps:

1. Be sure you are saved.
2. Confess your sins.
3. Surrender to Jesus afresh, and give Him the right to do whatever He wants in your life.
4. Tell Him you want everything He has for you.
5. Ask Him for the baptism (filling, sealing) with the Holy Spirit.
6. Allow Him to take control of your spirit-man—the inner you.
7. Respond to His move as He leads and endows.
8. Praise Him as He leads in His fullness and power.

Intimacy with Christ

From Adam and Eve's quiet walks in Eden recorded in Genesis to the amazing visions given to John in Revelation, God has sought a personal relationship with individuals. It is no mistake that God uses marriage terms throughout Scripture to help us understand the depth of His desire for us, such as "the bride of Christ" and "the marriage supper of the Lamb." Consider the implications of this verse: "Husbands, love your wives, just as Christ also loved the church and gave Himself for her" (Eph. 5:25 NKJV).

God wants to *know* us in a powerful, intimate way. Genesis 4:1 tells us Adam *knew* Eve his wife; God wants us not just to *perceive* His character, but to *experience* Him. The same Hebrew word for *know* is used in these passages:

> Those who do wickedly against the covenant he shall corrupt with flattery; but the people who *know* their God shall be strong, and carry out great exploits. (Dan. 11:32 NKJV, emphasis added)

> "But let him who glories glory in this,
> That he understands and *knows* Me,
> That I am the LORD, exercising lovingkindness, judgment, and
> righteousness in the earth.
> For in these I delight," says the LORD. (Jer. 9:24 NKJV, emphasis
> added)

God knew we could understand His love in a tangible way by relating it to our intimate natures. The consummation of the physical act of human marriage is an act of total surrender and unconditional devotion. In a similar sense, the baptism of the Holy Spirit is an act of total surrender of yourself to the power of the Spirit of God. It is no coincidence that many individuals have outward physical manifestations when they are filled with the Spirit, such as weeping, trembling, and the like, for this most intimate surrender to the Holy Spirit touches us at the core of our human emotions.

Don't be afraid of allowing God to establish a deeper relationship with you. Take a step today toward giving Him your unconditional surrender and love.

Chapter 3

A NEW
WINESKIN CHURCH

In Jesus' day, mankind's spiritual life was in big trouble. Judaism had descended into legalism, the Romans had their dead gods, and paganism had infiltrated the land. Jesus came in the middle of all that to bring vitality and true religion to a hungry people.

JESUS INITIALLY REJECTED

In my observation, rarely does the religious establishment embrace a new move of God. Whether historical or modern, God's divine visitations almost always face opposition and controversy. The fresh move of God may even be opposed by the old move of God.

The Lord Jesus Christ created the universe, wrote the Old Testament, and finally came into His world to rescue the perishing. Upon His arrival on the planet, His own covenant people did not recognize Him, much less welcome Him: "He came to His own, and His own did not receive Him" (John 1:11 NKJV).

His miraculous birth was questioned: "Is this not the carpenter's son?" (Matt. 13:55 NKJV). They even slyly claimed that He was illegitimate. Then they said to Him, "We were not born of fornication; we have one Father—God" (John 8:41 NKJV). His native state of Nazareth did not seem to be a likely launching pad for the Messiah they expected.

He had shown great promise as a twelve-year-old at His bar mitzvah, astounding the scholars in Jerusalem. Yet His continued insistence that God was His Father had raised a few eyebrows. He kept talking about being on a mission from His Father: "And He said to them, 'Why did you seek Me? Did you not know that I must be about My Father's business?'" (Luke 2:49 NKJV).

Eighteen years later Jesus would launch His ministry, not by attending the right schools and plugging in with the religious leaders in Jerusalem, but by giving His approval to the most extreme religious movement of the day. Jesus identified with the "fanatic" John the Baptist. Jesus' problems really began then. He dared to allow John to baptize Him, the same John who had called the leaders of the religious order a "brood of vipers!" (Matt. 3:7 NKJV).

Unusual happenings began to surround the ministry of Jesus: "The heavens were opened to Him, and He saw the Spirit of God descending like a dove and alighting upon Him. And suddenly a voice came from heaven, saying, 'This is My beloved Son, in whom I am well pleased'" (Matt. 3:16–17 NKJV). He soon was considered the enemy of the religious order of His day. The religious experts rejected Him.

If the incarnation and earthly ministry of Jesus were ridiculed and rejected by religion, why should we be so surprised when the same opposition arises in today's work of God? Jesus told a parable about God's fresh work:

No one puts new wine into old wineskins; or else the new wine will burst the wineskins and be spilled, and the wineskins will be ruined. But new wine must be put into new wineskins, and both are preserved. And no one, having drunk old wine, immediately desires new; for he says, "The old is better." (Luke 5:37–39 NKJV)

If individuals and churches are to experience the new wine of God's presence, then there must be a change of wineskins. The wineskin represents the structure that carries the fresh wine. These wineskins made of goatskin or sheepskin got old and useless when they were not cared for properly. Wineskins could stay new and pliable if they were rubbed with olive oil. Obviously, the wineskin pictured the religious establishment in Jesus' day and prophesied the church in our day. Only churches that are constantly rubbed and renewed by the anointing oil of the Holy Spirit can carry the new wine of God's fresh revelation of Himself and what He is doing.

To refuse the anointing of the Holy Spirit leaves the old wineskin church stiff and inflexible. The fermenting new wine bursts and destroys the old wineskin, and the new wine of God's movement is lost.

To put this in today's language, when a church resists the Holy Spirit and refuses to change, several tragedies are possible.

CHANGE RESISTED

It is very common to see the first tragedy: that of rejection to change. A church may reject the movement of God, preferring to stay in a comfort zone as members go through the motions of religion: "Having a form of godliness but denying its power. And from such people turn away!" (2 Tim. 3:5 NKJV).

The worst part of this tragedy is that these folk do not have a clue that they have missed God's visitation. They live in the past like Samson, who "did not know that the LORD had departed from him" (Judg. 16:20 NKJV). Or they live like Saul, who lost the power of the

Holy Spirit: "But the Spirit of the L ORD departed from Saul" (1 Sam. 16:14 NKJV).

Change is resisted because it often comes in the form of new people. The old leaders feel challenged as new life pours into the church. The fear of loss of control brings resistance. Change also tears up schedule and routine. Old liturgies and orders may go out the window as the Spirit of God is allowed to interrupt to have His glorious way. That is the wonderful thing about the Spirit-filled life; God can still surprise you. Jesus said to Nicodemus about the Holy Spirit, "The wind blows where it wishes, and you hear the sound of it, but cannot tell where it comes from and where it goes. So is everyone who is born of the Spirit" (John 3:8 NKJV).

THE BODY SPLINTERED

A second tragedy is that of a divided church. The old wineskin bursts under pressure. To put it more clearly, the church splits and splinters. People divide over small, picky points of doctrine, worship style, gifts of the Spirit, and supernatural manifestations. Some want tidy, compact church services that start at eleven o'clock sharp and end at twelve o'clock dull. Of course, the old wineskinners blame the new wine for bursting their church, never seeing the truth that it was their own inability to change that destroyed the church.

In the wake of Jesus' ministry, Judaism would never be the same. At His death, the temple veil was torn in two. That signified the end of temple worship: "Then, behold, the veil of the temple was torn in two from top to bottom; and the earth quaked, and the rocks were split" (Matt. 27:51 NKJV). The ripping of the veil was not an end, but a new beginning. It represented an invitation to intimacy with God. With the dawning of the new atonement in Jesus Christ, God cleared away the symbol of the old system. Israel has never been the same.

A number of the people who left our church as renewal broke out said, "We just don't know where this will end." The leadership had clearly stated both our mission and our purpose. The body had voted its approval of our direction. Those who left were really saying, "We don't like where the church is going. We were satisfied with the way things were."

No leader can predict the final destination of a move of God. A humble church in Florida has shown this to be true. More than 2.5 million people have visited Brownsville Assembly of God in Pensacola, Florida, since revival erupted on Father's Day in 1995. Now, years later, the revival continues with weekly meetings and/or prayer services, having seen nearly 140,000 decisions made for Christ.

No one at Brownsville Assembly had a clue that God was going to change the lives of millions of people through the church. Evangelist Steve Hill was unaware that his Father's Day speaking engagement at the church would turn into an extended preaching arrangement![1]

Predictability is not a part of God's plan. We must think big and dream big, realizing all the time, as Paul stated, that God is able "to do exceedingly abundantly above all that we ask or think" (Eph. 3:20 NKJV).

REVIVAL QUENCHED

The third tragedy is that the new wine will be lost upon the splitting of the old wineskin. In other words, the Holy Spirit will be quenched. When Jesus was rejected, Jerusalem was destroyed, and the people were scattered. Churches today that fight over the movement of God will often splinter and scatter. The new wine is lost and the hope of renewal vanishes. I observed this tragedy firsthand during my eight years as an officer with the North American Mission Board. I saw many churches in my denomination decline and die, while in the power of the Spirit they could have been growing.

THERE ARE OTHER OPTIONS!

Churches don't need to settle for the tragedies I've just described. The wineskin can refuse to get old by embracing constant renewal and change. As individuals are willing to accept the new move of God, the church will find itself renewed and flexible enough to recognize the new vision of God's visitation.

Sometimes the only option is for a new church to start out of the old. If forces against change are greater than forces that want change, then those in the renewal must leave and join or start a new wineskin church. As difficult as a split like this can be, we must remember that God orchestrates His work, and division could very often be one of His methods to enlarge a church's mission to reach more souls for His kingdom. Rather than see His people hunkering down behind the four walls of their church, bickering among themselves, He desires for them to reach out into a world of hurting people and draw them to Christ.

Sometimes the voices of change in a church will outnumber the forces of the past. Then the old wineskinners need to find a traditional church where they will be comfortable. Over the past three and a half years, our church has seen more than two thousand people join our body. Yet six hundred members have left. An inevitable part of growth is to suffer some loss. When a child loses her first tooth, it is not a disaster, only a sign of growth and change. The church will suffer some growing pains as God pours out His new wine upon the body.

A LESSON FROM HISTORY

The Great Awakening that took place in the early 1700s in New England was hastened to an early end by disagreements. Dividing into the "new lights" and "old lights," good friends split doctrinal and ecclesiastical hairs. Many preachers of the Awakening, such as

Jonathan Edwards, were distressed to see the division. They knew that such separation caused only senseless argument and literally hindered the work of God in their day.

NEEDED: A NEW WINESKIN CHURCH

In my own Baptist and evangelical community, the move of God's Spirit in my life and church has brought controversy, criticism, and cancellations. There is a fear of the renewal of spiritual gifts, the supernatural works of God, and the manifestations of revival. Yet many do not have a clue about reaching this present generation. Our churches must touch today's young adults in a powerful way.

The danger is that we will continue to minister only to a world of nostalgia. That approach will not work with today's generation. Consider what members of today's generation really want:

- They want personal relationships and will leave their big-screen TVs to find them.

- They want to participate and celebrate. They want to clap, raise their hands, and even dance before the Lord.

- When they are sick, they want to be touched and prayed for.

- They want their children trained to worship.

- Unlike the skeptical generation of the seventies, Generation X believes that demons and angels are real. Generation Xers want to know how to live in truth and freedom.

- They want a salvation that not only keeps them out of hell, but also helps them get up on Monday morning.

- They want a church that will follow Jesus in reaching the

poor and hurting and help people out of that lifestyle of despair.

- They want an intimate walk with Jesus Christ. Millions are looking for a church that does not want to exercise religious control, but desires to see great spiritual freedom.

Not long ago on a Sunday evening during one of our rocking worship services, God spoke to me and said, "Pray for the children." More than 1,500 people were present, and I had my sermon prepared. I said, "Okay, Lord." I asked children who felt a need in their lives to come forward for prayer. About one hundred school-age children soon crowded around me.

For more than an hour and a half I prayed with the children seated on the floor both on and around the platform. Several children fell out in the Spirit, and many wept and trembled under the power of God. Many who had not yet been saved came to Jesus. A number of the children were known to have attention deficit disorder (ADD), and yet they sat totally quieted and focused. Parents who could not control their children saw them absolutely calmed by the power of Jesus, and in the weeks to follow, some of these parents told me that doctors were able to remove their children from the drugs used to treat the disorder.

The children dispersed to their seats, and I thought I had finished praying. I looked to my left and saw thirty sets of Generation X parents who had gone to the nursery and picked up their small babies for prayer!

I learned that members of this generation want more than a sermon. They want the power of God on their lives and families. We need new wineskin churches filled with members who will listen to God, allowing the healing and changing power of His new wine to flow to the ones who desire it most.

Chapter 4

UNTANGLING
TONGUES

$\mathcal{I}$ was sure it could never happen to me.

As I lay before the Lord one night, praying for a pastor friend who was facing life-changing career decisions, I sensed something rising in my spirit-man. I felt wave after wave of joy in the presence of the Lord Jesus. The power of His presence soon issued in praise from my lips. As I prayed aloud, other syllables, strange to my mind, began to come, and I continued to speak them forth.

At the end of that season, I asked the Lord for an interpretation. He quickened my mind with a word of warning for my friend not to take the staff position he had been offered. I immediately phoned him with the word.

Within seven days, the pastor for whom he would have worked resigned. Had my friend gone into that position, he would have been left swinging in the breeze.

I was really in trouble. The unthinkable had happened to me. I had prayed in tongues! I began to remember all my sermons against what I called *glossolalia,* or speaking in tongues. *Glossolalia* sounded like something sinister or occult. I remembered railing against the charismatics and crudely referring to them as "charis-maniacs."

The biblical terms are nonthreatening in the Greek New Testament. *Glossa* means "tongues or language." *Laleo* means "to speak." Thus, *glossolalia* means "to speak in tongues or languages." *Charismatic* comes from the Greek *charismata*, which means "grace gifts." Several wonderful English words are related to the Greek word *charis: grace, Messiah, anoint,* and *joy,* to name a few.

My mind then began to think of people across the years of my ministry. In every church along the way, I remembered that some of my finest and most faithful members had told me of their own gift of tongues. None of them fit the picture of divisive or arrogant. Not one ever told me I was not saved or spiritually inferior because I disagreed with his position. They smiled a lot, prayed a lot, gave a lot, and never questioned my leadership or teaching.

Problems never arose from those Spirit-filled people; rather, the problems always came when *other* members began to fear the freedom that those people had in Christ. I had looked down on those folks as if they were not quite as biblically smart as I was. Yet not once had any of those precious people done anything to upset the church. They practiced their gifts quietly.

Over time, the Spirit proceeded to hem me in so that I had no choice but to consider the validity of these spiritual gifts. I remember my own daughter Heather going off with a group of charismatics at age fifteen. She had been in a season of rebellion in her life, but at the weekend retreat, she had a profound experience and returned home changed and empowered, wearing a big wooden cross around her neck. Instead of encouraging her new zeal and joy, I warned her not to hang around with that bunch of off-the-wall people. I pointed out that if she really wanted to exhibit a spiritual life, she would take part in the events of our own youth group and church.

Her response to my impressive lecture was a mumbled, "Whatever, Dad." She soon dropped out of church for years, until God brought renewal to my life.

My mind also recalled the day that a young woman, who now serves on my executive staff, came home from her university telling of her experience of renewal with the Holy Spirit. She was the godliest person who had come out of our youth group. Her experience shocked me, for I knew she did not have a phony bone in her body. She was real and I knew it. I felt that what had happened to her was very interesting, but I hoped she wouldn't tell anyone about it. Needless to say, she didn't bring up the subject around me.

So now, I had personally experienced the same blessing of God. I was faced with answering a serious question: Were all the great preachers, singers, songwriters, and ministers *faking* who had claimed this experience, or was it emotional excess? This question *had* to be resolved since God had released in me the one thing I had said I would never do: speak in tongues.

HAVE TONGUES CEASED?

For years I had thundered from the pulpit, "Tongues have ceased!" I based my position on 1 Corinthians 13:8. I had read all the standard cessationist interpretations. Now I was forced to look again at 1 Corinthians 13. It said, "Tongues will cease," in the future tense. This ceasing will happen when the "perfect" comes (1 Cor. 13:10 NKJV). Although a few believe this "perfect" refers to the close of the biblical canon or completion of the written Scriptures, I discovered that most scholars interpret "perfect" as a reference to the second coming of Jesus. When He comes, the necessity for all the spiritual gifts will disappear.

Billy Graham has recently rereleased his book on the Holy Spirit.

I was surprised to discover that Dr. Graham does not believe that tongues have ceased. He defines his view in this way:

> Although there is honest disagreement among Christians about the validity of tongues today, I personally cannot find any biblical justification for saying the gift of tongues was meant exclusively for New Testament times . . . Indeed, tongues *is* a gift of the Spirit . . . Today there are Presbyterians, Baptists, Anglicans, Lutherans, and Methodists, as well as Pentecostals, who speak or have spoken in tongues.[1]

Somehow it seems more comfortable for many Christians to believe that all of these spiritual manifestations have ceased than to worry about the modern church controlling the free expression of the gifts. Today we want an orderly church without the volatile and embarrassing disruptions brought on by an unleashed Holy Spirit. Listen to Michael Green:

> It is simply not the case that healing, prophecy, exorcism, and speaking in tongues died out with the last apostle. Still less can a passage like 1 Corinthians 13:8 ("as for prophecies, they will pass away; as for tongues, they will cease . . .") be used to attest the supposed demise of these gifts.[2]

You see, the gifts will pass away when the perfect comes at the Second Coming, not at the end of the apostolic age or after the formation of the New Testament canon, as some believe. There is plenty of evidence in the postapostolic days and periodically through church history to show that these gifts did not die out in the first century.

First Corinthians 1:4–7 (NKJV) demonstrates that Paul expected all the gifts to be in operation at the end of the age:

I thank my God always concerning you for the grace of God which was given to you by Christ Jesus, that you were enriched in every thing by Him in all utterance and all knowledge, even as the testimony of Christ was confirmed in you, so that you come short in no gift, eagerly waiting for the revelation of our Lord Jesus Christ.

Many scholars, such as Michael Green, Jack Deere, Michael Brown, and Wesley Campbell, cite the postapostolic material and historical references to an unbroken line of usage among some groups across the years. In a later chapter we will take a walk through history to see the evidence of the Holy Spirit through the ages.

THE VALUE AND USE OF TONGUES TODAY

The subject of tongues continues to cause debate among Christian scholars, but I believe that the Bible teaches that there are varied giftings of tongues. One of these giftings is a prayer language available to every Christian for individual edification, and the other is a prophetic gift of tongues given to a select few to edify the church body.

BUILDING UP THE BODY

The prophetic gift of tongues is often misused and misunderstood. Paul addressed the Corinthian Christians on this issue, for he was concerned that they esteemed the gift so highly that it threatened to overcome the other aspects of worship.

First Corinthians 14 records some strong cautions and careful guidelines for its use in public worship. In the gathered public church, the gift of tongues should be a rare occurrence. Paul limited its use to *three* times in a gathering and required that each speak separately. The guidelines further indicate an interpreter is required. If someone pronounces a message in a tongue during a service and no interpretation comes, the person should be commanded to keep silent.

The benefits of tongues when interpreted in a service can be great. The prophetic message can build up, encourage, and comfort others in the church, providing words of vision and expectation.

PRACTICING A PRAYER LANGUAGE

Though the prophetic gift of tongues may be of limited use in public worship today, its use for the individual believer is clearly taught in Scripture. In spite of all the precautions cited in 1 Corinthians 14 having to do with the practice of tongues, Paul strongly warned the enemies of freedom, "Do not forbid to speak with tongues" (1 Cor. 14:39 NKJV). And he declared, "I speak with tongues more than you all" (1 Cor. 14:18 NKJV).

In Gordon Fee's monumental work *God's Empowering Presence: The Holy Spirit in the Letters of Paul,* I was overwhelmed as I realized the depth of Paul's reliance on the supernatural work and power of the Holy Spirit.[3] Paul prayed and sang in the Spirit. The legalistic Pharisee who seemed so stern broke out in joy and freedom at his conversion. Even in describing the kingdom of God, Paul could hardly contain himself as he shouted, "The kingdom of God is not eating and drinking, but righteousness and peace and joy in the Holy Spirit" (Rom. 14:17 NKJV).

The benefits of a private prayer language are many.

COMMUNICATING IN JOY

The first benefit we see in tongues is that the gift releases joy in the believer's life. The gift of tongues allows one's spirit to communicate directly to God's Spirit: "For he who speaks in a tongue does not speak to men but to God" (1 Cor. 14:2 NKJV). This closeness of fellowship releases joy.

Many times when tongues are mentioned, we find that individuals also "magnify God," such as in Acts 10:46. When Mary exalted God in expectation of the birth of Jesus, she declared, "My spirit has rejoiced in God my Savior" (Luke 1:47 NKJV). The translation in Greek for this word literally means "jump for joy"! Although we don't know that Mary praised God in tongues, there was a literal move in her spirit in response to the joy of the Holy Spirit, who had overshadowed her in preparation for the coming of Jesus.

In our Western Christianity, we seem to be saturated by an approach to God based on Greek philosophy and rationalism rather than the power of the Holy Spirit. We have elevated education above the work of the Holy Spirit. I am not anti-intellectual and do not believe anyone should put his brain on the shelf when he comes to church. However, our minds are darkened and corrupt, and we are ever battling the natural man, or the flesh. Clearly, we are told, "The natural man does not receive the things of the Spirit of God" (1 Cor. 2:14 NKJV). In other words, our flesh fights things that are not explainable.

A spiritual realm exists whereby God communicates to the spirit and then to the mind. Only as we offer ourselves in brokenness and surrender can God renew our minds and reveal Himself to us.

PRAYING IN DISCERNMENT

Speaking in tongues may bring the capacity to understand some of life's mysteries: "In the spirit he speaks mysteries" (1 Cor. 14:2 NKJV). We often do not know how to pray, as we ought, but through the spirit, secrets can be revealed. In fact, we learn that the Spirit Himself prays for us, as revealed in Romans 8:26–27 (NKJV):

Likewise the Spirit also helps in our weaknesses. For we do not know what we should pray for as we ought, but the Spirit Himself makes intercession for us with groanings which cannot be uttered. Now He who searches the hearts knows what the mind of the Spirit is, because He makes intercession for the saints according to the will of God.

The Holy Spirit can pray for us when we do not know how to pray for certain needs. The Father knows our needs before we ask. I am convinced a person can be led of the Spirit to pray in his native language; however, God has also provided a language of prayer by which we may communicate spirit to Spirit with the Lord. Paul addressed this at length in 1 Corinthians 14:

For he who speaks in a tongue does not speak to men but to God, for no one understands him; however, in the spirit he speaks mysteries . . . He who speaks in a tongue edifies himself, but he who prophesies edifies the church . . . For if I pray in a tongue, my spirit prays, but my understanding is unfruitful. What is the conclusion then? I will pray with the spirit, and I will also pray with the understanding. I will sing with the spirit, and I will also sing with the understanding. (1 Cor. 14:2, 4, 14–15 NKJV)

Paul spent most of 1 Corinthians 14 addressing the need for interpretation to accompany tongues in public worship. However, he reminded the believers that there are great benefits to using tongues in private prayer. He encouraged them to use their gifts properly.

There is a mystery about prayer, which causes us to ask, Why do we need to pray if God is ever present and all-knowing? The answer is this: we pray not to inform God, but to adjust our lives to what He has already set in motion. It pleases God for us to pray. He has called us to intercession. He willed to operate only in answer to prayer. A person may pray with the Spirit or with the understanding. As we pray in the Spirit, God moves through us to pray for what our flesh could never comprehend.

In 1 Corinthians 4:1 (NKJV), we discover that we are "stewards of the mysteries of God." "Steward" translates the Greek word for "manager." As a manager, one must know how to get and transfer resources where they may be needed.

A hidden wisdom predates the creative order (1 Cor. 2:6–7). The wisdom was not some higher human knowledge revealed only to a select few, as some believe. It was a revelation of God's purpose revealed by the Spirit to the praying Christian.

As we open up the spirit-man to God, the Scriptures become more alive to us. The power of God is released. The Holy Spirit quickens the spirit and anoints us to receive the truth from God's Word. Instead of our learning Scripture as history or literature, the Holy Spirit gives us the capacity to grasp the "things of God" as we read the inspired Word of God. An anointing of understanding comes upon believers:

> The anointing which you have received from Him abides in you, and you do not need that anyone teach you; but as the same anointing teaches you concerning all things, and is true, and is not a lie, and just as it has taught you, you will abide in Him. (1 John 2:27 NKJV)

Paul had a working knowledge of the Old Testament before he was saved and filled with the Spirit. However, as Paul prayed in the Spirit and experienced the very presence of God, the Holy Spirit gave him a deeper understanding of the Scriptures. It is the same today; the Holy Spirit does not bring new truth, but brings new revelation of the truth already revealed in Scripture as we pray in the Spirit. We are heart-to-heart with God without the filter of our flesh.

This special revelation will cause you to stop in the middle of your reading of a Scripture passage and feel as though a verse is leaping off the page in bold clarity. The verse may seem to come alive to you and speak to you personally and directly.

STRENGTHENING THE SPIRIT

Prayer in the Spirit can strengthen the inner man. While the Holy Spirit freely uses a number of ways to encourage and fortify believers, prayer language is one means He uses to strengthen us. The primary use of tongues today is for personal edification, or the building up of the individual's spirit for ministry.

The following text is often cited critically to condemn tongues as a selfish gift: "He who speaks in a tongue edifies himself" (1 Cor. 14:4 NKJV). It is true that gifts are given to edify or build up the whole church as the body of Christ. However, the body is made up of individual members who need individual strength and blessing. In this verse, Paul told of the benefits of his prayer language and, as we already read in verse 15 of the same chapter, again emphasized his determination to continue the practice in his own life when he stated, "I will pray with the spirit, and I will also pray with the understanding." He knew that the corporate body is only as strong as its individual members, and that he must privately continue to exercise a gift that God specifically gave him to strengthen him in ministry.

If I play on a football team, would I be considered selfish for taking part in personal training in order to build up my strength? Would I be selfish because I exercised and lifted weights? Of course not, for my individual strength would be added to the team's strengths. A prayer language can strengthen the inner man. Paul prayed for his fellow believers to learn this truth so that they may "be strengthened with might through His Spirit in the inner man" (Eph. 3:16 NKJV).

This strengthening includes a confirmation of the faith, what we believe, as well as the ability to exercise faith in the work of God. Listen to Jude: "Building yourselves up on your most holy faith, praying in the Holy Spirit" (Jude 20 NKJV).

This building up includes releasing the ability to publicly prophesy or proclaim the Word of God. The gift of tongues stirs up the prophetic gift. In 1 Corinthians 14:5 (NKJV) the text reveals, "I wish you all spoke with tongues, but even more that you prophesied." Listen to that phrase, "but even more that you prophesied." The English translations don't communicate the full effect of the original Greek. If you investigate this verse word for word in any of the excellent concordances or interlinear Greek texts, you'll find that this is the more literal translation: "I would that you spoke with tongues *much* in order that you may prophesy *greater*."

In later writings, Paul would say that five understood words are better than ten thousand in tongues when those tongues cannot be clearly interpreted. We should also consider that a person ought to pray ten thousand words privately in his closet before he speaks before the people of God. As I go early to my office on Sunday morning before I step out to preach to the church body, I find I must spend time exercising my prayer language. It is in no way a mere ritual; rather, it builds up my spirit and stimulates the prophetic gift in me so that I can speak His Word with boldness.

WORSHIPING IN TRUTH

Tongues can also be a form of worship for the believer. Paul confessed to singing in the Spirit as well as praying in the Spirit. In Acts 10:46 (NKJV), it is recorded that "they heard them speak with tongues and magnify God." On the day of pentecost both a miracle of speaking and a miracle of understanding occurred. The apostles spoke in ecstatic utterance, and many dialects were understood.

If you picture the scene at pentecost, you would have to admit this occurrence likely did not include prophetic, interpreted tongues. Thousands of people had gathered to investigate what had happened to the apostles. A mighty wind was howling through the room at the same time that all the loud voices of the apostles were praising God in tongues. Yet above all the noise, people heard in their own languages the tongues at pentecost giving praise to God!

This incident seems to involve a miracle of hearing as well as understanding because no interpreter is mentioned in the book of Acts. Tongues were useful for worship and praise in the presence of believers. Though I don't wish to say God cannot work as He chooses, I feel Scriptures indicate that for the most part, when tongues are used in public worship, an interpreter is required.

SOME CAUTIONS ABOUT TONGUES

We must be aware that demons can counterfeit tongues. Just as people can be influenced by demons to make false professions of faith, so can Satan transform himself to appear as a minister of righteousness.

Avoiding tongues because of misuse is not necessary, however. We would never consider giving up preaching because some people responding to the sermons make phony decisions.

The simple answer to this caution is to obey 1 John 4:1–2 and test the spirit by asking the person to privately pray in tongues in the presence of a mature believer. The counselor can ask the spirit praying in tongues to confess Jesus as Lord in English. I have seen the gift of tongues verified many times in this manner.

On some occasions, though, I have heard the demonic imitation. While I was preaching in another city, I was distracted during an altar call by a woman who was crying out loudly, bending over. I sensed it was a disruption, so I proceeded to test the spirit. She responded to the test by crying, "Jesus is *a* lord." I replied, "Is He your Lord?" The demon in her answered me, screaming, "No, He is not my Lord." Subsequently, we cast the demon out of the woman and led her to Christ. She was a leader and a worker in her church, and yet she had a false tongue.

Beware of the counterfeit gifts given by demons. Satan counterfeits only what is valuable. Human counterfeiters aren't interested in counterfeiting pennies. They counterfeit valuable currency. Likewise, demons want people to receive a phony substitute for the true power of God.

A second caution is to avoid spiritual pride. Though many godly men claim so, a person does not have to have the gift of tongues as an evidence of the power and anointing of the Holy Spirit. Don't try to force your gift on others, and humble yourself in the hand of God who gives gifts as He chooses.

As stated earlier, caution must be used when tongues are exercised in a public worship service. The guidelines given in 1 Corinthians 14 should be followed, and an interpretation should always occur. The pastor or leader should exercise discretion because demonic imitation of prophetic words could cause spiritual confusion in the church.

The habit of many well-meaning believers of coming up behind inquirers during an invitation and praying in tongues should stop. It could distract the unsaved from hearing the gospel. Your prayer language should not be exercised in the presence of the uninformed, so that you do not cause confusion or division.

It is the task of the pastor to preach and teach the church. It is never appropriate to interrupt the teaching and preaching of God's Word by an individual either in tongues or in a natural language.

Primarily because of the misuse and abuse of tongues, division and misunderstanding have arisen over the years. A believer with this gift should be careful of the context in which he exercises the gift. Using this gift around people who are unfamiliar with and uninformed of its use would not be loving or appropriate.

After saying all this, I must carefully state that I would not presume to limit God's working, but I caution you as a believer to be sensitive to the Holy Spirit.

Do You Have the Gift of Tongues?

A study of Scripture reveals that speaking in tongues was likely the most common gift practiced by believers in the early church. It was definitely the first sign gift released in the early church. How can you recognize and release this gift in your own life?

1. You will have a desire for intimacy with the Lord.

2. You will sense your spirit-man and the Spirit of God desiring to communicate.

3. The Holy Spirit will rise within you, and your spirit-man will speak through vocal cords.

4. You must exercise your will. You must choose to speak by opening your mouth and allowing the language of heaven to pour forth.

5. Your spirit will learn this language, and you will be able to speak this language at will. Furthermore, you can stop speaking at will.

If you don't receive this gift, do not fret or feel inferior. God may desire to release other gifts in you. Later, God may give you this gift as well.

A FINAL WORD

Those who speak in tongues are not better than those who don't. Don't criticize the gift or be jealous of those who have it. Be grateful for all the gifts in the body of Christ. One of the greatest blessings in the Christian life is the diversity of gifts in believers. As God's power rests on each of His children, the body reaps the benefits.

The church today has no need to chase after signs such as tongues. Jesus promised that these and other signs would follow as believers' hearts grow hungry (Mark 16). Remember, saving lost souls is our goal. We must be balanced, not bigoted, toward tongues.

Part 2

REDISCOVERING THE BIBLE

Chapter 5

IS THE GOD OF MIRACLES STILL PRESENT?

Gideon said to Him, "O my lord, if the LORD is with us, why then has all this happened to us? And where are all His miracles which our fathers told us about?" (JUDG. 6:13)

Standing in my traditional Baptist church, I sang as a new convert with all the strength and fervor that my eight-year-old vocal cords could muster. I truly believed that "He Lives" and that He gives "Peace Like a River."

Furthermore, as a boy, I had no doubt that Jesus was in my heart. I had experienced His power firsthand. Later, I would learn more about the objective trust that supported my experience, yet the experience itself remained a vivid pillar of my faith. I had encountered not just the Bible, but the One whom the Bible declares to be the Living Word, Jesus Christ.

TRUTH VS. EXPERIENCE

The evangelical world today divides doctrine into two camps, calling its own doctrine "truth based" and calling charismatic doctrine "experience based." There are several problems with this division.

First, there can be no valid Christian doctrine without experience. Scripture was not dictated to a scholar sitting in an office. Scripture was the inerrant, Holy Spirit–inspired witness of men to the mighty acts of God! Some Scripture actually came through the ministry of angels. Other passages were given to men while they were in an ecstatic state. As we will see in a later chapter, even the apostle Paul's life was changed not by having an encounter with scholarship, but by being knocked down by the Holy Spirit. We must remember that Jesus spoke of a balance in life, a need to operate *in Spirit and in truth.*

Second, the Scriptures themselves validate personal encounters with Jesus Christ and the Holy Spirit. Without a doubt the Bible speaks of and *encourages* personal encounters with God. For many, the Bible has become an icon or an idol. In their error, the Book becomes larger than its Author. The pathway to Christ becomes a destination of its own. Deep Bible study replaces the vital experience of knowing Christ.

Paul felt that salvation was just like a resurrection. He wrote, "And you He made alive, who were dead in trespasses and sins" (Eph. 2:1 NKJV). The goal of the Christian life to Paul was not greater knowledge of the Hebrew Old Testament, his Bible. The goal was to *know Christ:* "That I may know Him and the power of His resurrection, and the fellowship of His sufferings, being conformed to His death" (Phil. 3:10 NKJV).

Third, evangelical tradition and theories are often lifted higher than Scripture. One such tradition is cessationism, which teaches that all of the miracles and supernatural gifts ceased sometime during the early church age. One aspect of this belief argues that the gifts were uniquely given for a time to fulfill the promise given in Acts 1:8 (NKJV). At that time, the apostles were promised power as they ministered in "Jerusalem, and in all Judea and Samaria, and to the end of the earth." Some hold the argument that once tongues were revealed in each of these places, they were retracted, and the promise was fulfilled. However, there remain parts of our world that do not know the gospel, so how could this promise be completed?

Others who hold to cessationism argue that the gifts ceased when the last apostle died. Mark 16:17–18 (NKJV) contradicts this belief because Jesus promised that signs and wonders would follow "those who believe." Still others insist the gifts came to an end when the canon of Scripture was completed. Unfortunately, they cannot cite an exact date for this occurrence, since there is much debate about when the canon was actually closed, and argument continues about the Apocrypha, which some insist should have been included in our Bible.

Yet another separate theory called dispensationalism concerns the dividing of Scripture into ages. This theory is a man-made system. Furthermore, a theory continues to survive that teaches there are only three periods of miracles in all of history, which we will discuss further in this chapter. All of these theories and ideas are often elevated to the same plane as the holy Scriptures.

Many have made the false accusation that our brothers and sisters in the renewal movement base all of their beliefs on *experience* without the authority of Scripture. This accusation is obviously unfounded when one reads the carefully indexed works of Jack

Deere, Michael Brown, Jon Mark Ruthven, and other scholars. Their studies are meticulously documented with Scripture.

WERE THERE ONLY THREE PERIODS OF MIRACLES?

Evangelical embarrassment over the supernatural dates back to the Reformation. Calvin, Luther, and Zwingli railed against both the papacy and what is called the radical reformation. Baptists, Methodists, Church of God members, Assemblies of God members, Congregationalists, and others have roots in this so-called radical reformation. Luther, at best, arranged the New Testament to fit his theology and, at worst, denied the biblical authority of the supernatural in much of the New Testament. He even rated certain books in the New Testament above others. Jon Mark Ruthven cites Luther's "Preface to the New Testament," in which Luther elevated the books of Romans, Galatians, Ephesians, and 1 Peter as "the true and noblest books." Luther's sole criterion for selecting these books as superior was that they did not contain any descriptions of supernatural works or miracles.[1]

Building upon this approach that demeans much of Scripture, evangelical scholars have sectioned off the Bible into acceptable and nonacceptable Scriptures. Unlike the position of the classic liberal, who denies all the miracles in Scripture, the trend today is to categorize them as past events. In this way, the "problem" of supernatural manifestations is quietly disposed of. Historical tradition has robbed today's church of supernatural power.

The theory that claims the existence of only three periods of miracles in the Bible has been popularized in our day by popular Bible teacher Dr. John MacArthur in his book *Charismatic Chaos*. In MacArthur's view, God performed miracles only in three brief periods when He was inspiring Scripture.[2] Jerry Vines, in his book *Spirit Life*, also supports this view.[3] The problem with this view is that it is totally without biblical support.

According to this theory, miracles happened only from the period of Moses to Joshua (during the giving of the Law), in the period of Elijah and Elisha (giving us the prophets' writing), and in the period of Christ and the apostles (during the forming of the New Testament).

Author Jack Deere, on the other hand, has pointed to the miracles that took place outside these three special periods of revelation. Deere counters the skeptics by listing the miracles that were performed outside the supposed three periods, the number of which is absolutely overwhelming![4] Let us take our own walk through the Bible to examine the supernatural events that took place during the "gaps" between the supposed periods of miracles.

MIRACLES IN THE OLD TESTAMENT

After reading some scholars, you would expect to find no miracles outside their three defined periods. All of the weird stuff should be isolated only to these periods and not disturb the rest of history, right? Wrong! Let's start in Genesis, where we find the following:

- The miracle of creation (Gen. 1)

- The rapture of Enoch (Gen. 5:24)

- The Flood (Gen. 6–8)

- The Babel experiences (Gen. 11)

- The call of Abram (Gen. 12:1–3)

- Abram's trance, the smoking fire pot, and the blazing torch (Gen. 15)

- An angel appears to Hagar (Gen. 16:7)
- The destruction of Sodom (Gen. 19)
- Lot's wife turned into a pillar of salt (Gen. 19)
- The miraculous birth of Isaac (Gen. 21)
- The angel prevents Abraham's killing of Isaac (Gen. 22)

That is only half the book of Genesis, dating to about 2000 B.C. Looking at the rest of the Old Testament, if the miracles are confined to the three periods, then we see the following:

- All of the miracles in the lives of Jacob and Joseph recorded in Genesis are eliminated.
- All of the miracles in Judges performed by Samson don't count.
- Hannah's miracle birth of Samuel must go.
- King Saul's encounter with the Holy Spirit is irrelevant.
- David's miraculous victory over Goliath can't be possible.
- All of the miracles in Daniel aren't needed.

Do you get the picture? Our miracle-working God does not fit in a man-made theory. His supernatural power explodes across all the pages of Scripture.

DID MIRACLES CEASE WITH THE APOSTLES?

Those who believe that the miracles and some of the gifts of the Spirit ceased at the death of the last apostle base their theory on these points: (1) Miracles happen purely to validate new doctrine; (2) miracles happen only at times when God is inspiring Scripture; and (3) those who believe in supernatural power and gifts today are accused of elevating their experiences to a level equal with the inspired Scriptures. These are false assumptions and accusations.

Where did this idea of the cessation of miracles and gifts arise? Cessationist theories go back to Calvin, Luther, and Zwingli. The Reformers, reacting to the false miracle reports by Roman Catholicism, such as the figure of the Virgin Mary appearing on a wall, and also their fear of the fringe groups such as Anabaptists, launched them to react to the supernatural.

The Reformers and their successors today teach that miracles rarely happen anymore. We must look to theologian B. B. Warfield's *Counterfeit Miracles*, written in response to the rise of pentecostalism in the early part of this century, as the foundation of today's argument. What Warfield lacked in biblical support, he seemed to make up for with dogmatic assertion of his theories. Warfield accepted that "general supernatural acts" including healing might happen, yet he felt they could not truly be called miracles. He further proceeded to divide "spiritual gifts" into ordinary and extraordinary. Again, that view has no biblical support. Warfield used the same arguments that liberals use when they attack the miracles of the Bible, even as he proceeded to attack those who believe miracles still happen today.

Even more distressing was Warfield's intellectual arrogance, for he stated that "right-thinking" people (or people in their right minds!) would clearly understand that miracles don't happen in this age, as if the natural man could ever perceive the things of the Spirit.[5] As a matter of fact, the Scripture explains why Warfield and many of his fellow theologians could not come to terms with the supernatural: "But the natural man does not receive the things of the Spirit of God, for they are foolishness to him; nor can he know them, because they are spiritually discerned" (1 Cor. 2:14 NKJV).

Miracles were not given as proofs; rather, they were a revelation of God and His character. Make no mistake; when God's kingdom breaks through today, there will still be supernatural manifestations.

THE BIBLE ANNIHILATES CESSATIONISM

Both 1 Corinthians 1:4–8 and 1 Corinthians 13:8–13 teach that the gifts of the Spirit and the supernatural works of God will continue until the second coming of Jesus Christ. The Holy Spirit is God's promise to every believer: "Then Peter said to them, 'Repent, and let every one of you be baptized in the name of Jesus Christ for the remission of sins; and you shall receive the gift of the Holy Spirit. For the promise is to you and to your children, and to all who are afar off, as many as the Lord our God will call'" (Acts 2:38–39 NKJV).

The miracle of pentecost does not need repeating. Yet its promise is mine. Down to this very age, the Holy Spirit's benefits are available to you and me.

As we journey through the book of Acts, we find verification of the promise of the Spirit. In Acts 8:14–17 (NKJV), the Gentiles received the power of the Holy Spirit:

> Now when the apostles who were at Jerusalem heard that Samaria had received the word of God, they sent Peter and John to them, who, when they had come down, prayed for them that they might receive the Holy Spirit. For as yet He had fallen upon none of them. They had only been baptized in the name of the Lord Jesus. Then they laid hands on them, and they received the Holy Spirit.

In Acts 10:44–48 (NKJV) the gentile household of Cornelius received the Holy Spirit, including a manifestation of tongues, astounding the Jews:

While Peter was still speaking these words, the Holy Spirit fell upon all those who heard the word. And those of the circumcision who believed were astonished, as many as came with Peter, because the gift of the Holy Spirit had been poured out on the Gentiles also. For they heard them speak with tongues and magnify God. Then Peter answered, "Can anyone forbid water, that these should not be baptized who have received the Holy Spirit just as we have?" And he commanded them to be baptized in the name of the Lord. Then they asked him to stay a few days.

In Acts 15, Paul and Barnabas defended their ministry among the Gentiles, basing this defense on the pentecostal promises:

So God, who knows the heart, acknowledged them by giving them the Holy Spirit, just as He did to us, and made no distinction between us and them, purifying their hearts by faith . . . Then all the multitude kept silent and listened to Barnabas and Paul declaring how many miracles and wonders God had worked through them among the Gentiles. (Acts 15:8–9, 12 NKJV)

In Acts 19:1–7 (NKJV), Paul ministered to some disciples in Ephesus who were previously untaught. They received the Holy Spirit with gifts and a release of supernatural power:

And it happened, while Apollos was at Corinth, that Paul, having passed through the upper regions, came to Ephesus. And finding some disciples he said to them, "Did you receive the Holy Spirit when you believed?" So they said to him, "We have not so much as heard whether there is a Holy Spirit." And he said to them, "Into what then were you baptized?" So they said, "Into John's baptism." Then Paul said, "John indeed baptized with a baptism of repentance, saying to the people that they should believe on Him who would come after him, that is, on Christ Jesus." When they heard this, they were baptized in the name of the Lord Jesus. And when Paul had laid hands on them, the Holy Spirit came upon them, and they spoke with tongues and prophesied. Now the men were about twelve in all.

And consider Acts 19:11–12 (NKJV): "Now God worked unusual miracles by the hands of Paul, so that even handkerchiefs or aprons were brought from his body to the sick, and the diseases left them and the evil spirits went out of them."

Jesus would chide this church at Ephesus for leaving their first work and first love while remaining orthodox (Rev. 2). I believe Jesus was calling them to a return to supernatural power.

Immediately, a cessationist will say, "You cannot get doctrine from the book of Acts!" I find this objection repeatedly mentioned in cessationist literature. To this I respond, Where does the Scripture say to ignore the book of Acts for teaching? The Bible as its own witness says, "All Scripture is given by inspiration of God, and is profitable for doctrine, for reproof, for correction, for instruction in righteousness" (2 Tim. 3:16 NKJV).

Yes, even the book of Acts can be used to instruct the church.

A CALL TO THE CHURCH

Finally, let us look at some concluding passages. Paul chided the Galatian Christians not to forsake the power of the Spirit for the works of their own flesh:

O foolish Galatians! Who has bewitched you that you should not obey the truth, before whose eyes Jesus Christ was clearly portrayed among you as crucified? This only I want to learn from you: Did you receive the Spirit by the works of the law, or by the hearing of faith? Are you so foolish? Having begun in the Spirit, are you now being made perfect by the flesh? Have you suffered so many things in vain—if indeed it was in vain? Therefore He who supplies the Spirit to you and works miracles among you, does He do it by the works of the law, or by the hearing of faith? (Gal. 3:1–5 NKJV)

Today we have elevated our fleshly theories above Scripture. In Romans 11:29, Paul declared that the charismatic gifts will not be taken away. "Gifts" here is the Greek *charismata*. In the verse, Paul stated, "For the gifts and the calling of God are irrevocable" (NKJV). *The Living Bible* reveals the same verse in this way: "For God's gifts and his call can never be withdrawn; he will never go back on his promises."

Paul further warned us: "Having a form of godliness but denying its power. And from such people turn away!" (2 Tim. 3:5 NKJV). *The Living Bible* paraphrases the thought: "They will go to church, yes, but they won't really believe anything they hear. Don't be taken in by people like that." I am convinced that today's church needs all the gifts and power of God. Cessationism at best is an excuse for the church's lack of power and the awful absence of Jesus' presence.

In Paul's teachings on the gifts, each gift had a crucial place in the body: "And the eye cannot say to the hand, 'I have no need of you'; nor again the head to the feet, 'I have no need of you.'" (1 Cor. 12:21 NKJV). Today's cessationist would mutilate the body of Christ by cutting off the supernatural gifts.

Even if there must be disagreement, can there not be tolerance at least among those who hold to the inerrancy of Scripture? Appalling ugliness and intolerance can be viewed on all sides of this controversy. The charismatic teacher of healing, Dr. F. F. Bosworth, was forced to resign from his own Assemblies of God denomination because he could not embrace "evidential tongues," the belief that tongues were *required* at the filling of the Holy Spirit as a proof that it actually took place. Bosworth, who wrote the classic *Christ the Healer,* truly believed in tongues as a gift and a prayer language. Yet he believed the Bible taught that a Christian could be baptized in the Spirit without experiencing tongues. After enduring much criticism and ill will from fellow ministers, this great man took a stand and left his denomination.[6]

Today Baptists and some evangelical groups want to dismiss from the fellowship people they perceive as charismatic. Recently, a large denominational body dismissed two of their most effective missionaries in the Pacific region from their posts following a "manifestation" of supernatural works of the Spirit in their churches. The previous year, they had led more than 1,500 souls to Christ!

Jesus rebuked the intolerance of His own followers:

Now John answered Him, saying, "Teacher, we saw someone who does not follow us casting out demons in Your name, and we forbade him because he does not follow us." But Jesus said, "Do not forbid him, for no one who works a miracle in My name can soon afterward speak evil of Me. For he who is not against us is on our side." (Mark 9:38–40 NKJV)

The war must end between truth and Spirit. A marriage of these two will not bring uniformity, but it will bring an incredibly powerful unity. Jesus is alive today and must be released to do His complete ministry in the church.

Let us always rejoice over the work that God does personally and lovingly in the heart of every Christian who isn't afraid to release His Spirit to work in freedom.

Chapter 6

THE REAL JESUS

The people answered Him, "We have heard from the law that the Christ remains forever; and how can You say, "The Son of Man must be lifted up? Who is this Son of Man?" (JOHN 12:34 NKJV)

Herod said, "John I have beheaded, but who is this of whom I hear such things?" So he sought to see Him. (LUKE 9:9 NKJV)

Jesus Christ is the central personality of all time and eternity. He refuses to fit in any man-made box. The beautiful artwork of the Middle Ages does not adequately represent His person. He is earthly and unearthly at the same time. Though fully man, He is also fully God.

The Western church has caricatured Jesus into an Anglo-Saxon suburban Protestant in a three-button suit. We have fashioned a Jesus who fits our contemporary thinking. He has been placed into the image of European Reformation theology and Scholasticism rather than Someone from the dusty roads of the Middle East. We have pressed the grid of our own comfort zone upon His ministry. Voices from today's evangelical leadership dare to state what Jesus can and cannot do.

When Jesus entered Jerusalem, the entire city was stirred and asked the question of the ages, "Who is this?" (Matt. 21:10 NKJV). Today there is little disagreement concerning His virgin birth, His divine nature, His humanity, His vicarious death, His bodily resurrection, His present heavenly session as intercessor, and His soon return. Furthermore, there is little argument among evangelicals that in order to be saved, a person must receive Jesus Christ as Savior and Lord.

However, looking honestly at the New Testament, we must confess that Jesus was far more than we have understood and embraced. My conclusion is that Jesus would not fit in the average Baptist or evangelical church. He would be outside our understanding and beyond our comfort zone.

I believe Jesus' ministry would embarrass the average 11:00 A.M. Sunday worship crowd. This Jesus we have invented is a quiet, introspective evangelical who wants people to be saved, but we are not sure from what or for what. The Jesus we've invented has left an emptiness that causes people to have to take pills to get up and pills to go to bed. He does not lay hands upon the sick or drive out devils. No, this Jesus gives people a ticket out of hell and then supposedly a somewhat cleaned-up new life.

The evidence rails against the common view of conversion. Our people are depressed, unbalanced, miserable, defeated, and ineffective in their personal struggles. We heap more guilt on them by declaring the joys of our innocuous Christ-filled life, but we leave them struggling in their own flesh to find it. Having stripped Jesus of His right to do supernatural works in our day, we face a people trying vainly to live a Christ-filled life without supernatural power.

Look honestly at your life, and ask yourself, Where is the power of God? How is it displayed in my life?

AN EMBARRASSING JESUS

The Jesus of the New Testament had His entry into life heralded by the ministry of angels. Angels visited His aunt, His mother, and His father. You want to raise some eyebrows in your church? Start talking about angelic visitation and ministry in your life. Begin to speak of dreams and visions, and see the response that you get.

Suppose you could walk back into Jesus' day and could ask Him to explain His work. He would respond,

"The Spirit of the LORD is upon Me,
Because He has anointed Me
To preach the gospel to the poor;
He has sent Me to heal the brokenhearted,
To proclaim liberty to the captives
And recovery of sight to the blind,
To set at liberty those who are oppressed;
To proclaim the acceptable year of the LORD." . . .
And He began to say to them, "Today this Scripture is fulfilled in
your hearing." (Luke 4:18–19, 21 NKJV)

All this talk about the Holy Spirit coming upon Him and this idea of anointing would immediately make Him suspect. Jesus' language sounds strangely charismatic.

Jesus would speak of how He existed long before He arrived in the manger bed: "Before Abraham was, I AM" (John 8:58 NKJV). Then He would ask you to believe His mother was a virgin when He was born.

Jesus would talk about His life on earth. He would declare His purpose:

For the Son of Man has come to seek and to save that which was lost. (Luke 19:10 NKJV)

For this purpose the Son of God was manifested, that He might destroy the works of the devil. (1 John 3:8 NKJV)

God anointed Jesus of Nazareth with the Holy Spirit and with power, who went about doing good and healing all who were oppressed by the devil, for God was with Him. (Acts 10:38 NKJV)

On our visit back to Jesus' day, He would have us follow Him across the dusty roads of Galilee. As we watch Him, we would be amazed at His power over nature.

- He turns water into wine (John 2:1–11).
- Jesus stills the howling storm (Mark 4:35–41).
- Jesus walks on water (John 6:16–21).
- Jesus miraculously catches fish (John 21:1–14).
- Jesus causes a fig tree to wither at His word (Mark 11:12–24).
- Jesus fetches money from the mouth of a fish (Matt. 17:27).
- Jesus feeds five thousand once and four thousand on another occasion supernaturally (John 6:5–14; Matt. 15:32–39).

We would then walk with Jesus into the realm of the sick and infirm.

- Jesus heals Peter's mother-in-law (Mark 1:30–31).

- Jesus cures the incurable (Mark 1:40–45; Luke 14:1–6).

- Jesus restores a withered hand (Mark 3:1–5).

- Jesus opens the eyes of the blind (John 9:1–7).

- Jesus restores hearing and speech (Mark 7:31–37).

- Jesus allows the physically disabled to walk again (John 5:1–9).

We continue to follow Jesus to the funeral home and graveyard.

- Jesus raises Jairus's daughter from the dead (Luke 8:41 56).

- He raises the widow's son from the dead (Luke 7:11–17).

- With the family looking on, Jesus raises Lazarus from the dead (John 11:38–44).

Jesus then leads us into the realms of darkness and evil.

- He delivers a demoniac from a legion of demons (Mark 5:1–13).

- He sets free a boy from an evil spirit (Mark 9:14–27).

Finally, Jesus speaks of His death and describes for us the pain, agony, and blood of the Cross. Then He tells us that He fights an invisible war whereby He disarms "principalities and powers" and He makes "a public spectacle of them, triumphing over them in it" (Col. 2:15 NKJV).

Jesus then asks us to understand that His salvation was far more than a ticket out of hell or a formula to make us feel good. He explains that He came to rescue us, to deliver us from the powers of the enemy: "He has delivered us from the power of darkness and conveyed us into the kingdom of the Son of His love" (Col. 1:13 NKJV).

Isn't it amazing what He suffered for us!

JESUS COMES TO OUR CHURCH

Imagine if Jesus were a guest speaker in the average church. First, ever the good Samaritan, He may be running slightly late, having stopped to help a family stranded by the side of the road. When He finally arrives, He catches some cold stares from folks lingering in the vestibule. They notice He isn't wearing a suit and tie, but the work clothes of a carpenter.

We hurry Jesus to the pastor's office where we hand Him our bulletin. With a smile at the corners of His lips, He gives our printed order of service a glance and says, "We will see."

The choir begins the call to worship, and we walk in with Him. Suddenly, several individuals begin to scream and cry out, "Jesus, why have You come to torment us?" They fall at His feet, writhing and crying out. Everyone stares at the scene, trying to guess what Jesus will do. Will He deal with such things in *church*?

Jesus gazes around at the crowd, His eyes sweeping over the audience as if searching out every needy soul. He speaks again the words He once read in a synagogue,

The Spirit of the LORD is upon Me,
Because He has anointed Me
To preach the gospel to the poor;
He has sent Me to heal the brokenhearted,
To proclaim liberty to the captives

And recovery of sight to the blind,
To set at liberty those who are oppressed;
To proclaim the acceptable year of the LORD." (Luke 4:18 NKJV)

Turning to the persons still writhing at His feet, Jesus casts out the demons, "Come out of them." The delivered people lie quietly in the aisles of the church. Suddenly, the sick begin streaming toward Him for His touch. He lays hands on them, and they begin to leap and shout, praising God for their healing.

Jesus quiets the crowd and begins to teach with authority, and sinners weep under conviction. Before a formal invitation can begin, they fall prostrate at the altar and are gloriously saved.

Word soon spreads to the children's church that Jesus is in the building, and they leave behind their craft projects and Sunday school papers to find Him. With noisy enthusiasm, the children burst through the sanctuary doors. Embarrassed parents reach out to restrain them as they try to run to Jesus, clamoring for His touch, but Jesus says, "Let the little children come unto Me." He touches all of them with a blessing.

Young people gather around Him next, begging to follow Him as disciples. He asks them if they are willing to take up His cross. Will they go anywhere? Dozens volunteer!

Soon, the aged saints with youth still in their hearts come, asking, "Is it true we will have a body like Yours?" He smiles at them and tells them of the glorious victory they will have over the grave. He blesses them for their faithfulness and charges them to continue their mentoring of the younger saints. They step back from His words with hope restored, feeling a new vigor to go on and serve Him as long as they live.

Then suddenly, a woman with the marks of the world on her countenance begins weeping loudly. Her face is tear-streaked with makeup that never could hide the ravages of immorality. She falls at his feet, covering them with tears as she receives His pardon.

On another side of the building, music begins to sound, and a dad and his son are dancing in the aisles. We hear the dad cry, "This my son was dead and is alive again. He was lost and is found."

By this time the leaders are gathering in the back, watching. One says, "I cannot believe our pastor brought this radical into our church." Another replies, "We better get this back in hand quickly." Another speaks, "Some of our best people have left upset today."

I ask you, Does the real Jesus dare show up in our churches?

Too many churches have learned how to operate without Jesus, much like the end-time church of Laodicea. No doubt the Lord makes this same lament over our day,

> I know your works, that you are neither cold nor hot. I could wish you were cold or hot. So then, because you are lukewarm, and neither cold nor hot, I will vomit you out of My mouth. Because you say, "I am rich, have become wealthy, and have need of nothing"— and do not know that you are wretched, miserable, poor, blind, and naked . . . Behold, I stand at the door and knock. If anyone hears My voice and opens the door, I will come in to him and dine with him, and he with Me. To him who overcomes I will grant to sit with Me on My throne, as I also overcame and sat down with My Father on His throne. (Rev. 3:15–17, 20–21 NKJV)

Jesus' presence should be evident today in our services through the ministry of the Holy Spirit. Churches will be different when He shows up in full power! Today the church is a colony of heaven. We are outposts of another kingdom beyond time and space. These outposts should be expressions of Jesus' presence and power. The power of the world to come must be evident in our churches. The powers of heaven can be ours through the earnest or down payment of the Holy Spirit. The supernatural should be normal in the life of the church.

WWJD: What Would Jesus Do?

From Thomas à Kempis's *Imitation of Christ* to the wonderful novel by Charles Sheldon entitled *In His Steps,* Christians have been encouraged to try to imitate Jesus. This imitation has primarily to do with the character of Jesus. Bracelets, key chains, and necklaces bearing the initials WWJD have become hot sellers in the past two years, especially among students. A schoolteacher in our church commented that when she asked her students wearing the bracelets to explain the initials, two out of three had no clue what they stood for.

Of course, we don't have to ask what Jesus would do *if* He were here! Jesus Christ *is present* with us today by the Holy Spirit. We don't have to imitate Jesus; we have His life in us. Does it not follow that Jesus' ministry could also flow out of us today?

The church is Jesus' bride, body, and building. He is her Lord, Head, and Source. In 1 Corinthians 1:4–8 (NKJV), we discover what the testimony of Jesus Christ should be like in today's church:

> I thank my God always concerning you for the grace of God which was given to you by Christ Jesus, that you were enriched in every thing by Him in all utterance and all knowledge, even as the testimony of Christ was confirmed in you, so that you come short in no gift, eagerly waiting for the revelation of our Lord Jesus Christ, who will also confirm you to the end, that you may be blameless in the day of our Lord Jesus Christ.

Do we have to conjure up His presence? No, these verses tell us that He is already here. Paul explained the implications:

- Today's church was given the "grace of God" by Jesus Christ (v. 4). "Grace" is akin to the Greek *charis,* referring to all the endowments of the Spirit.

- These "riches" have resulted in an outpouring of the Word and knowledge (v. 5).

- How was the testimony of Christ confirmed and substantiated (v. 6)? By the evidence of the gifts (charismata) of the Spirit (v. 7).

- This evidence will still be present at the second coming *(apokalupsin)* of our Lord Jesus Christ (v. 8).

The testimony of Jesus is for the church today. He gives us grace, enriches us in everything, conforms us, and gifts us so that we will not be wanting at His return. Jesus is returning not for a ragged beggar, all worn out and barely making it, but for a bride living, lovely, and longing for Him. He is returning not for the church mediocre, but for the church militant. Let us prepare the bride for His coming!

Chapter 7

WAS PAUL A CHARISMATIC?

*U*nion with Christ was the heart and soul of Paul's faith. Jesus Christ was not simply Paul's Savior; He was Paul's life. Proof of his devotion can be found throughout his writings: "For to me, to live is Christ" (Phil. 1:21 NKJV); "When Christ who is our life appears" (Col. 3:4 NKJV); and "It is no longer I who live, but Christ lives in me" (Gal. 2:20 NKJV).

For Paul, Christ was not a passport to heaven, but the Friend of all friends with whom he was in vital union: "He who is joined to the Lord is one spirit" (1 Cor. 6:17 NKJV).

The Holy Spirit governed and controlled Paul's life. You will be overwhelmed by the multiple references to the Spirit in Paul's letters. The late James S. Stewart, former chaplain to the queen of England, spoke of Paul's spiritual union with Christ in his wonderful book *A Man in Christ:*

> Until we realize the central place which this always held in Paul's thought and experience, many of the richest treasures of his gospel must remain sealed from our sight . . . Union with Christ . . .

means the steady unbroken glory of a quality of life that shines by its own light, because it is essentially supernatural.[1]

The Holy Spirit dominated Paul's life. Most Christians today understand what Christ has done "for us," but they may not have a clue concerning what He wants to do "in us." In Paul, salvation was more than a formula or a plan. Salvation was no less than an invasion or a takeover of one's life by the spirit of Jesus:

> But God demonstrates His own love toward us, in that while we were still sinners, Christ died for us. Much more then, having now been justified by His blood, we shall be saved from wrath through Him. For if when we were enemies we were reconciled to God through the death of His Son, much more, having been reconciled, we shall be saved by His life. (Rom. 5:8–10 NKJV)

A SUPERNATURAL CONVERSION

Paul was a Christ-captured, Spirit-filled man with everything in his Christian life rooted in experience. Yet he was an unlikely candidate for conversion to Christ. Listen to his self-description in Philippians 3:

> Though I also might have confidence in the flesh. If anyone else thinks he may have confidence in the flesh, I more so: circumcised the eighth day, of the stock of Israel, of the tribe of Benjamin, a Hebrew of the Hebrews; concerning the law, a Pharisee; concerning zeal, persecuting the church; concerning the righteousness which is in the law, blameless. But what things were gain to me, these I have counted loss for Christ. Yet indeed I also count all things loss for the excellence of the knowledge of Christ Jesus my

Lord, for whom I have suffered the loss of all things, and count them as rubbish, that I may gain Christ and be found in Him, not having my own righteousness, which is from the law, but that which is through faith in Christ, the righteousness which is from God by faith. (vv. 4–9 NKJV)

We must not take lightly the background of Paul. To him, religion was a taskmaster that drove all of his effort. The law was Paul's life and love. He was a Pharisee of noble birth and high order. He could trace his lineage to Benjamin, one of Jacob's favorite two sons. Paul's life was deeply rooted in the faith to which he was called to propagate and protect.

There are three accounts of Paul's conversion in Acts (Acts 9; 22; 26). In those accounts, Paul mentioned the goads that pushed him toward Christ. Goads were pointed pieces of wood on the back of a plow designed to wound the animal that kicked at its master. God supernaturally placed some goads into his life that Paul kicked at until he was saved. Dr. James S. Stewart listed some of the goads:

1. One of the sharpest and most stinging goads was the failure of his religion, Judaism. If anything was obvious in Paul, it was the fact that religion to him was toil and stress. Yet he was so committed to it that he had people killed to protect it.

2. Another goad was the fact of the historic Jesus. It was Paul's task before his conversion to disprove the claims of the would-be Messiah. To do that, he traveled about and heard the eyewitness testimony of many.

3. A difficult fact for Paul to deal with was the holiness in the lives of the Christians. Even as the Christians were dying, Paul saw their peace in the midst of their martyrdom.

4. Finally, the way Stephen died made an impression on Paul. Acts records that Paul held the garments of the murderers of Stephen. It is reasonable to assume that Paul was also present to hear the message of the young deacon given just before his stoning.[2]

In Acts 7, Stephen preached a passionate address, declaring the reality of the supernatural God to the legalists.

- This God appeared to Abraham (vv. 2–3).
- This God gave Abraham a child miraculously (vv. 4–8).
- This God set Joseph over Egypt (v. 9).
- This God preserved Moses in the Nile (vv. 20–21).
- This God spoke to Moses by an angel out of the burning bush (vv. 30–34).
- This God brought Israel out with signs and wonders (v. 36).

Paul did not know this miracle-working God whom the young Spirit-filled Stephen so boldly described. Later, as the dark night of death descended on Stephen at his stoning, instead of cries of pain and curses of vengeance, Paul heard these words: "Lord Jesus, receive my spirit . . . Lord, do not charge them with this sin" (Acts 7:59–60 NKJV).

All of those events stripped away Paul's pride and exposed his empty heart. He continued his murderous threats against the church until a miracle completely captured him personally. Luke related the story:

As he journeyed he came near Damascus, and suddenly a light shone around him from heaven. Then he fell to the ground, and heard a voice saying to him, "Saul, Saul, why are you persecuting Me?" And he said, "Who are You, Lord?" Then the Lord said, "I am Jesus, whom you are persecuting. It is hard for you to kick against the goads." So he, trembling and astonished, said, "Lord, what do You want me to do?" Then the Lord said to him, "Arise and go into the city, and you will be told what you must do." And the men who journeyed with him stood speechless, hearing a voice but seeing no one. Then Saul arose from the ground, and when his eyes were opened he saw no one. But they led him by the hand and brought him into Damascus. And he was three days without sight, and neither ate nor drank . . . And Ananias went his way and entered the house; and laying his hands on him he said, "Brother Saul, the Lord Jesus, who appeared to you on the road as you came, has sent me that you may receive your sight and be filled with the Holy Spirit." Immediately there fell from his eyes something like scales, and he received his sight at once; and he arose and was baptized. (Acts 9:3–9, 17–18 NKJV)

MIRACLES AT PAUL'S CONVERSION

Look with me at the miracles surrounding Paul's salvation:

- A supernatural light appeared from heaven (Acts 9:3).
- Paul and the company fell under the glory (Acts 9:4).
- Paul heard the voice of Jesus (Acts 9:4–6).
- Paul was struck blind (Acts 9:8).
- Ananias had a vision that instructed him to go to Paul (Acts 9:10).
- Paul had a vision that a man would come to heal his blindness (Acts 9:11–12).

- Ananias laid hands on Paul, and he received his sight and was filled with the Holy Spirit (Acts 9:17–18).

Paul's conversion was powerful and surrounded by supernatural wonders.

PAUL'S EARLY MINISTRY

Many Christians have a salvation testimony that is nothing short of miraculous, but they refuse to admit that God can still perform wonders in their lives after their conversion. In Paul's life, the supernatural events taking place in his life increased after his spiritual birth:

- In Acts 13:8–12, Paul struck Elymas with blindness for opposing the words.
- In Acts 14:3, signs and wonders confirmed the message of Paul at Iconium.
- Paul healed a disabled man at Lystra (Acts 14:8–10).
- Paul was nearly killed, but miraculously survived a stoning at Lystra (Acts 14:19–20).
- At the Jerusalem council, Paul reported "many miracles and wonders" (Acts 15:12).
- Paul subsequently saw a vision and in that vision received the call to Macedonia (Acts 16:10).
- Paul cast a demon out of a young woman at Philippi (Acts 16:18), and he was arrested and jailed as a result.
- While Paul sat in that jail cell, God sent an earthquake and opened the jail doors, resulting in the jailer's salvation (Acts 16:25–34).

- Paul had another vision at Corinth that encouraged his ministry because the vision promised many converts (Acts 18:9–10).

- Paul ministered to the followers of John the Baptist in Ephesus, and he saw people being saved, speaking in tongues, receiving unusual miracles, being healed by the touch of fabric that had been touched by Paul, and being delivered from demons (Acts 19:4–6, 11–13).

- Paul's ministry continued in power as God raised young Eutychus from the dead (Acts 20:9–12).

- Paul experienced the Lord standing by him in the night and speaking to him (Acts 23:11).

- The words and ministry of angels surrounded Paul (Acts 27:23–24).

- Paul was preserved from snakebite on the island of Malta (Acts 28:3–6).

- On the same island, Paul healed the father of Publius, in addition to many others (Acts 28:8–9).

It is clear that Paul walked in the supernatural power of God.

THE TESTIMONY OF PAUL'S LETTERS

Paul defined the kingdom of God as "righteousness and peace and joy in the Holy Spirit" (Rom. 14:17 NKJV). He further declared that Gentiles are made obedient "in mighty signs and wonders, by the power of the Spirit of God" (Rom. 15:19 NKJV). Paul spoke of the revelation of the Spirit of God and "the deep things of God" (1 Cor. 2:10 NKJV). He declared that he spoke in tongues more than they all did (1 Cor. 14:18). He taught that there are gifts of miracles and healings (1 Cor. 12:9–10).

As we look at more of Paul's letters, we discover that God gives supernatural strength for suffering, even when He chooses not to spare us (2 Cor. 12). God's preserving power is upon the believer until his work is done (2 Cor. 1:10). In spite of struggles we are always led "in triumph" (2 Cor. 2:14 NKJV). Our source of life is not the letter of the law, which "kills"; rather, the "Spirit gives life" (2 Cor. 3:6 NKJV). Every believer is being transformed "from glory to glory, just as by the Spirit of the Lord" (2 Cor. 3:18; Gal. 3:14–15 NKJV).

Furthermore, a supernatural God enables us to war on Satan and his stronghold (2 Cor. 10:1–6). He provides us with weapons of the Spirit (Eph. 6:10–18). By the Spirit we disarm the enemy (Col. 2:15).

Revelation and vision were common to the apostle (2 Cor. 12:1–2; Eph. 1:17). Also, Paul declared that all of the signs of an apostle followed him, included signs, wonders, and mighty deeds (2 Cor. 12:12). These signs and wonders followed not only the apostles, but also everyone who believes, as Jesus promised,

> These signs will follow those who believe: In My name they will cast out demons; they will speak with new tongues; they will take up serpents; and if they drink anything deadly, it will by no means hurt them; they will lay hands on the sick, and they will recover. (Mark 16:17–18 NKJV)

Even in Paul's defense of the gospel to the church at Galatia, he appealed to the supernatural:

> O foolish Galatians! Who has bewitched you that you should not obey the truth, before whose eyes Jesus Christ was clearly portrayed among you as crucified? This only I want to learn from you: Did

you receive the Spirit by the works of the law, or by the hearing of faith? Are you so foolish? Having begun in the Spirit, are you now being made perfect by the flesh? Have you suffered so many things in vain—if indeed it was in vain? Therefore He who supplies the Spirit to you and works miracles among you, does He do it by the works of the law, or by the hearing of faith? (Gal. 3:1–5 NKJV)

LIFE BY THE SPIRIT

Every aspect of the Christian life is to be governed by an ongoing fullness of the Holy Spirit (Eph. 5:18). Paul's preaching came not "in word only, but also in power, and in the Holy Spirit" (1 Thess. 1:5 NKJV). Later Paul warned the church "Do not quench the Spirit" (1 Thess. 5:19 NKJV). All of Paul's letters validate the supernatural power of the Holy Spirit.

WOULD PAUL BE WELCOME IN YOUR CHURCH?

Paul was a man who prayed for the sick, spoke in tongues, used prayer cloths, cast out demons, and experienced visions, dreams, and trances. Yet this man shook the Western world for Jesus Christ.

You may be saying, "Well, all those things stopped with the apostles." Once again, I must point out that this belief is pure speculation with no solid biblical support. Throughout this book, Scriptures are listed that clearly give evidence that the gifts will be in operation until the second coming of Christ.

The charismatic gifts will be just as active at the end of the age as they were at the beginning. These gifts will both confirm and strengthen the believer as the end of the age draws near.

The Scriptures teach that tongues and other gifts will be unnecessary in heaven:

Charity never faileth: but whether there be prophecies, they shall fail; whether there be tongues, they shall cease; whether there be knowledge, it shall vanish away. For we know in part, and we prophesy in part. But when that which is perfect is come, then that which is in part shall be done away. When I was a child, I spake as a child, I understood as a child, I thought as a child: but when I became a man, I put away childish things. For now we see through a glass, darkly; but then face to face: now I know in part; but then shall I know even as also I am known. And now abideth faith, hope, charity, these three; but the greatest of these is charity. (1 Cor. 13:8–13 KJV)

When the "perfect" comes, then there will be no necessity for the gifts. The perfect is not the canon of Scripture, but the coming of Jesus. After His coming, we will no longer need the gifts of our infancy, nor will we need the *charismata* as a mirror of the power of the world to come. We will be in heaven, in the ultimate place of His presence. In heaven, we will know fully what the gifts of the Spirit only gave us a glimpse of. Just as God now knows us, we will know Him. In addition, faith and hope will end, for faith will become sight and hope will be realized. Love never ends.

Cessationism as a doctrine gives the dead church an excuse for its lack of power.

WHAT PAUL WOULD SAY TODAY

If Paul could address our congregations today, his message would be unchanged. He would first pray for the church to be empowered:

For this reason I bow my knees to the Father of our Lord Jesus Christ, from whom the whole family in heaven and earth is named, that He would grant you, according to the riches of His glory, to be strengthened with might through His Spirit in the inner man, that Christ may dwell in your hearts through faith; that you, being rooted and grounded in love, may be able to comprehend with all the saints what is the width and length and depth and height—to know the love of Christ which passes knowledge; that you may be filled with all the fullness of God. Now to Him who is able to do exceedingly abundantly above all that we ask or think, according to the power that works in us, to Him be glory in the church by Christ Jesus to all generations, forever and ever. Amen. (Eph. 3:14–21 NKJV)

Second, he would warn us not to grieve the Spirit by ignoring the prophetic word. The Spirit has sealed us until the Second Coming. The words we speak are grace gifts, charismatic words offered to the believer. Our failure to speak forth words from God by His gifting grieves the Spirit of God, as we see in Ephesians 4:29–30 (NKJV): "Let no corrupt word proceed out of your mouth, but what is good for necessary edification, that it may impart grace to the hearers. And do not grieve the Holy Spirit of God, by whom you were sealed for the day of redemption."

Third, Paul would make this appeal to us: "Do not quench the Spirit. Do not despise prophecies. Test all things; hold fast what is good" (1 Thess. 5:19–21 NKJV).

These appeals are simple. We are not to put out the fire. We are not to despise the prophetic word. Here is a call to freedom for the believer. Paul felt it was important to have the gifts and words tested, yet he would not have them despised, quenched, or forbidden. By every standard of measurement, Paul would be suspect in many churches—and perhaps even unwelcome.

Billy Graham wrote,

According to Paul, the gifts . . . come from the sovereign operation of the Spirit of God, ". . . distributing to each one individually as He wills" (I Corinthians 12:17). The Spirit distributes gifts to the various members of the body. Thus, *every* believer gets some gift. And every believer is therefore a charismatic.[3]

If you are ever tempted to reject other believers because of the unusual workings of the Holy Spirit in their lives, take a moment to consider the principles laid out in Scripture. Just think, if the apostle Paul came into your church preaching on the fullness of the gifts of the Spirit, how would he be received?

Part 3

REREADING HISTORY

Chapter 8

THE NAZARETH
MENTALITY

*A*s I took the journey out of spiritual death to life, I noticed a resistance in the church immediately. A certain mentality held that everything had to be a certain way according to our tradition. Long-standing church leaders did not know the difference between Scripture and structure, between truth and tradition. I found that almost any person or church "going on" with God was facing opposition. If laypersons would look at their church records, they would see that a strong majority of evangelical churches are declining in growth, giving, attendance, and baptisms.

INSIDE THE COMFORT ZONE

The reason for this death in church ministry is irrelevant to many people. Too many churches are locked in a 1950s mentality and refuse to change to meet the needs of this generation. The average church does not want to move out of its comfort zone to touch today's world. Churches must take down their Do Not Disturb signs if they expect to survive. Christian people seem to sidestep anything messy, and revival *is* messy!

Proverbs 14:4 (NKJV) makes a practical observation of life: "Where no oxen are, the trough is clean; but much increase comes by the strength of an ox." You see, oxen mess up the barn. That was the high cost the Old Testament farmer had to pay in order to have animals available to help in planting and harvesting.

Revival and growth are often messy. We should keep in mind this proverb, and remember that where there is life, there will be evidence of life, and life can make things messy.

In Luke 4:16–30, Jesus messed up the religious barn. He exposed an attitude that I call "the Nazareth mentality." Jesus was the speaker in His home church in Nazareth. He selected Isaiah 61:1–2 (NKJV) for His text:

> The Spirit of the Lord God is upon Me,
> Because the Lord has anointed Me
> To preach good tidings to the poor;
> He has sent Me to heal the brokenhearted,
> To proclaim liberty to the captives,
> And the opening of the prison to those who are bound;
> To proclaim the acceptable year of the Lord.

While acknowledging the power of Jesus' words, the men of His community had rejected His supernatural claims. This process of thinking has survived in our church to this day. All was well in the synagogue service that day until Jesus closed the Scripture and said, "Today this Scripture is fulfilled in your hearing" (Luke 4:21 NKJV).

RESISTING THE MIRACULOUS

The first mark of this Nazareth mentality is that people operate as though the Word of God is either for the past or for the future. However, the members of this generation do not want a new word; they want a *now* word. They want the word applied to their lives. Unfortunately, those who maintain the Nazareth mentality love to talk about the miracles of the Bible or the great things that will happen in the future, but they resist the thought of any of those things happening today.

Why do some resist the thought of signs and wonders occurring in today's world? I know many friends who believe God is *able* to do a miracle in our day, but don't feel He has done one in recent times. I sense that many of them fear that if they embrace miraculous events such as healing, supernatural provision, and protection, they must embrace other "untidy" things, such as casting out demons or raising the dead. They resist the thought of losing control of the typical order of events in their lives.

AVOIDING THE OUTSIDER

Second, people with the Nazareth mentality don't want much to do with people who are not "like us." If others don't share our racial, denominational, cultural, or social background, they often disturb us.

When Jesus spoke a *now* word, it caused an uprising. Jesus knew that throughout biblical history, men had difficulty in accepting ministry that was unusual, and He pointed that out:

> Then He said, "Assuredly, I say to you, no prophet is accepted in his own country. But I tell you truly, many widows were in Israel in the days of Elijah, when the heaven was shut up three years and six months, and there was a great famine throughout all the land;

but to none of them was Elijah sent except to Zarephath, in the region of Sidon, to a woman who was a widow. And many lepers were in Israel in the time of Elisha the prophet, and none of them was cleansed except Naaman the Syrian." (Luke 4:24–27 NKJV)

When Jesus finished speaking those words, the crowd was "filled with wrath" and proceeded to try to throw Him off a cliff! The people wanted nothing to do with the idea that God might want to reach beyond the borders of their comfort zone to do His ministry.

In much the same way, when a minister begins to believe that God can still move today, cross-cultural ministry should happen in our churches, miracles can take place in our day, and the sign gifts are still valid, often his ministry becomes dangerous to the status quo. He may not be brought to the edge of a cliff by an angry mob, but many pastors have lost their church positions as a result of their belief in the power and gifts of the Holy Spirit for today.

DISCREDITING THE OBVIOUS

A third mark of the Nazareth mentality is that it would rather investigate than celebrate the works of Jesus. The Nazareth folk questioned the origin of Jesus and were offended by His claims:

Now it came to pass, when Jesus had finished these parables that He departed from there. When He had come to His own country, He taught them in their synagogue, so that they were astonished and said, "Where did this Man get this wisdom and these mighty works? Is this not the carpenter's son? Is not His mother called Mary? And His brothers James, Joses, Simon, and Judas? And His sisters, are they not all with us? Where then did this Man get all these things?" So they were offended at Him. But Jesus said to them, "A prophet is not without honor except in his own country and in his own house." Now He did not do many mighty works there because of their unbelief. (Matt. 13:53–58 NKJV)

When God begins to move, there exists a group that insists on investigating every act of God in order to discredit the supernatural.

In John 9, the man born blind was miraculously healed. He stood before the Pharisees with clear, healthy eyes, and yet they rejected the obvious. With the miracle staring them in their faces, they could not accept it because it cut across their legalistic mentality.

DENYING THE TRUTH

Last, this mentality reduces Jesus instead of reverencing Jesus. They called Him "Joseph's son" (Luke 4:22 NKJV). It is safe to assume that rumors of Jesus' virgin birth had spread throughout Nazareth and the neighboring areas. However, leaning back on their human understanding, they didn't acknowledge it as a supernatural birth, as John recorded in his gospel. The Nazareth mentality had spread to Jerusalem, for when Jesus was discussing their sin problem with them, they responded, "We were not born of fornication; we have one Father—God." Jesus replied, "If God were your Father, you would love Me, for I proceeded forth and came from God; nor have I come of Myself, but He sent Me" (John 8:41–42 NKJV).

Today the same mentality denies Jesus' supernatural work through His new body, the church. Miracles, signs, and wonders are still offenses to religion. The Jesus of many churches is minimized in size and effectiveness.

Churches that determine to serve a living, powerful Jesus will grow. A church enlarges its ministry through faith in Jesus. How big is Jesus in your church? Oh, how much we need the real, full-size Jesus in our church today!

WAVING BYE TO JESUS

As we study the Gospels, we find that Jesus' works were thwarted and He chose to move on from Nazareth. Even today He will not stay in an atmosphere of restrictive, prejudicial, religious legalism. Jesus will move on to a people of faith if we reject His work.

Some years ago while attending a conference, I listened to Leonard Sweet, futurist and dean of theology at Drew University, tell of his dreams for a future church that communicates powerfully to today's world. He told how he felt we were currently trying to minister to the world that we *wish* we had rather than the one we've *actually got*. Sweet called for a church of Spirit-driven leaders who dare to be "dangerously Christian." I recall his words of warning to mainline evangelicals about our work, expressing his fear that churches are not getting "fresh water" from the spiritual wells anymore. He saw the church complacently drawing from the aqueducts of our ancestors, using water that may be stale, even toxic, to today's generation.

We've got a whole world out there that is thirsty in the rain. People are hungry for an authentic move of God's power on their lives. The church must be renewed, or our members will go where their needs can be met. We must realize that today's generation longs for a church where the living Jesus is welcomed.

Chapter 9

BAPTISTS AND
OTHER HERETICS

Some years ago I heard the legendary coach Bear Bryant tell the following story. One day while Coach Bryant was speaking to the team, an unshaven older man dressed in overalls and a straw hat came to the door of the room and stood nervously looking around. Finally, Coach Bryant asked, "Sir, can someone here help you?"

The man replied, "I've come to see my boy who plays for you."

The embarrassed boy went over and acknowledged his dad and introduced him to Coach Bryant. Coach Bryant honored the man and treated him as if he were royalty. Later he called the boy in and said, "Son, don't ever be ashamed of your roots. No matter how humble they may be, your hardworking papa is part of the reason you are the man you are today."

I fear that as Baptists and evangelicals, we may often be unaware of our roots, and if we were aware of them, perhaps we would stand ashamed and embarrassed by them. Somehow we want to be accepted by the religious establishment and the intelligentsia. We don't want to talk about our past. In fact, we now want to *be* the religious establishment. We certainly don't want to be reminded of our emotionalism and revival fervor.

Somehow we have embraced a rewriting of the history of our spiritual roots. We like to present ourselves as linked to the great Reformers rather than to the zealous and persecuted Anabaptists. We look down on what we call the fringe elements of Christianity without remembering that our origins lie in the fringe. Nevertheless, as you study the workings of the Holy Spirit in your life, it is important to observe how Christians through the ages practiced biblical principles.

Baptists were birthed not in the quiet cradle of ritual, but in the burning fire of pentecost; however, the fire, the signs, the wonders, and the power of the Spirit now embarrass us. It is easier to say that these things have passed and mold our services into carefully orchestrated, orderly worship. Some evangelicals today have become self-appointed "bishops" responsible for making sure all the churches are in lockstep. The autonomy of the local church is threatened by an invisible code watched over by the guardians of tradition. Those who believe that all of the New Testament gifts and graces are for today are viewed as suspect, and they are accused of being non-Baptist or nonevangelical in practice.

Let's look back at our history as Baptists and evangelicals and see where we came from. By observing their practice of biblical truth, maybe we will learn where we should be going.

BAPTIST ROOTS

If you go to the standard commentaries printed prior to the twentieth century, you will search in vain for a clearly stated cessationist view. However, you *will* find that the supernatural gifts and miraculous things waned during the Middle Ages. You will also learn that the basic doctrine of justification by faith was not even embraced, much less the gifts, signs, and wonders brought on by the anointing of the Holy Spirit, except among the fringe elements of Christianity. At the so-called conversion of Constantine, the church became a patron of the state and lost its vitality. Descending into a dark night of ritualism and clerical professionalism, the church lost its soul.

To say that God no longer operates in power today by pointing to the dry spiritual season of the Middle Ages is to give validity to that time of spiritual decline. However, the Reformation brought a recovery of truth. The Reformation views of *sola fide* (by faith alone) and *sola scriptura* (the Bible alone) opened the door for a recovery of truth and of spiritual power. John Calvin and Martin Luther led the fight to return the church to the saving doctrines of the faith.

During the Middle Ages, an itinerant preacher and scholar visited the Vatican. After his tour, the priest who guided him said, "No longer does the church have to say, 'Silver and gold have I none!'" The visitor replied, "Neither can you say, 'In the name of Jesus rise up and walk!'" The loss of power during the Middle Ages was as tragic as the loss of truth.

Even during that dark time some fringe groups tried to maintain New Testament Christianity. The Church of Rome often viewed those groups as heretics. Baptists and evangelicals find their roots among those fringe groups. Baptist roots reach back beyond the Reformation and find their identity with the fanatical fringe.

Baptist historians, including Henry Vedder, generally agree that the people now called Baptists have been known by different names in different ages and countries. Vedder explains how the name Baptist was a contemptible title that was derived from the name given to our ancestors: the Anabaptists, or rebaptizers. That name was given to them because they insisted on baptism by immersion and refused to adopt the practice of infant baptism or sprinkling.[1] Baptist theologians, trying to rewrite history, tend to ignore this historical connection because some of the leaders of those fringe movements became heretical. However, Vedder admits that the possibility of a connection could exist: "One cannot affirm that there was not a continuity in the outward visible life of the churches founded by the apostles down to the Reformation . . . A succession of the true faith may indeed be traced, in faint lines at times, but never entirely disappearing."[2]

In Armitage's *A History of the Baptists,* the title page displays the following introduction:

A HISTORY OF THE BAPTISTS
TRACED BY THEIR VITAL PRINCIPLES FROM THE TIME
OF OUR LORD AND SAVIOR JESUS CHRIST
TO THE YEAR 1886.[3]

Other distinguished leaders in the last century, such as Dr. William Williams, once professor of church history at Southern Seminary, and Rev. George Gould of England, author of a series of Baptist manuals, declared the New Testament origins of Baptist life.

Zwingli, the Swiss Reformer, firmly declared in his "Reply to Wall" that Anabaptists were no novelty, but claimed that they had for 1,300 years been causing great disturbance in the church. He made that statement in 1530, showing that he felt the movement dated to A.D. 230.

In hatred, Zwingli also claimed Baptists were a part of the Waldenses' movement. Peter Waldo was a Frenchman born in 1150 who found himself hungering after God's Word. He hired someone to translate parts of the Latin Bible into the vernacular of the day, and as God's truth broke over his spirit, he had an intense desire to share it with everyone. He began preaching in the countryside, and the people were eager to finally hear God's Word in their language. Soon a number of lay preachers joined him who also spread the gospel through the land, and the Roman church became angry at those men who were preaching outside the authority of the established church.

More than the breach of authority upset the church fathers. Waldo and his converts believed in salvation by grace through faith in Christ, without the decrees of the church. They also believed that baptism was for adults who made a confession of faith, and they discouraged infant baptism. They believed there was no such thing as purgatory. Looking back through history, we find that later Anabaptists were most prevalent in areas where the preachers of the Waldenses were ministering just one or two centuries before.[4]

The Catholic church called these Baptist forebears heretics. Millions of them were tortured and murdered.

It has been our stated belief across the years that we are a part of an unbroken chain of churches called by various names that are the genuine practitioners of New Testament faith. We have believed, as stated, that we go back to the New Testament for our origins. For their own desire to be New Testament churches, loyal to the biblical faith, our forebears were banished, tortured, drowned, harassed, and mocked—all for a belief that New Testament practices remained valid in their day. Though I cannot write about every group, let's take a closer look at one of the earliest sects.

THE MONTANISTS

Around the middle of the second century, Montanism appeared and flourished in the greater part of Asia Minor. Though some called it a heresy, W. A. Jarrell in his *Baptist Church Perpetuity*, published in 1904, declared the Montanists to be forebears of Baptists, thus tracing our origin back to around A.D. 150. Said Jarrell, "Montanism enrolled its hosts and was one of the greatest Christian influences throughout the early Christian centuries."[5]

He stated further, "As there was at that time, when Montanism arose, no essential departure from the faith . . . the subjects of baptism, church government, or doctrine, the Montanists on these points were Baptists."[6] Though Montanus was accused of claiming to be the Comforter, he simply believed that a man could be filled and directed by the Holy Spirit.

Tertullian, perhaps the greatest preacher of the third century, embraced Montanism's doctrines, and his remarkable ministry gave evidence of the power of God. Tertullian refuted most of the attacks on Montanus, exposing those attacks as lies. The Montanists were millennialists, believing in a literal end-time one-thousand-year reign of Christ on earth, and held the Bible to be literally true. They had women teachers among them, and some even practiced triune immersion, but some may dispute these minor points. Tertullian believed that the Holy Spirit was the restorer of the apostolic model.[7] Möller, a noted church historian, commented on Tertullian: "To him the very substance of the church was the Holy Spirit not the Episcopacy [rule by bishops]." Jarrell observed, "Thus, in church government they were Baptists."[8]

Neander, yet another historian from the nineteenth century, wrote,

> Montanism set up a church of the Spirit . . . like Protestantism, [Montanism] places the Holy Spirit first, and considers the Holy Spirit first, and considers the church as that which is only derived . . . The gifts of the Spirit were to be dispersed to Christians of every condition and sex without distinction . . . to give prominence once more to the idea of the dignity of the universal Christian calling, of the priestly dignity of all Christians.[9]

Montanists experienced ecstatic worship, visions, prophecies, and the exercise of all the gifts of the Spirit. One young convert of Montanus described this ecstasy by saying, "On the wings of a dove I was carried above."

Jarrell quoted Dr. Thomas Armitage, who explained a key factor connecting Baptists with the Montanist beliefs:

> The one prime idea held by Montanists in common with Baptists, and in distinction to the churches of the third century was, that the membership of the churches should be confined to purely regenerate persons; and that a spiritual life and disciplined life should be maintained without any affiliation with the authority of the State. Exterior church organization and the efficacy of the ordinances did not meet their idea of Gospel church existence without the indwelling Spirit of Christ; not in the bishops alone, but in all Christians. For this reason Montanus was charged with assuming to be the Holy Spirit, which was simply a slander.[10]

Dr. William R. Williams in his *Lectures on Baptist History* said of the Montanists, "It was hard to find any doctrinal errors in their views; that they were rather like Methodists and Jansenists in their high views of religious *emotion and experience.* They were accused of claiming inspiration when they intended . . . the *true experience of* God's work in the individual soul." Dr. Williams continued, "They insisted much upon the *power of the Spirit* as the great conservator and guardian of the life of the Christian church."[11] Montanism was a reaction of Spirit-filled people to a church structure that moved in fleshly power and human manipulation rather than the power of the Holy Spirit.

Jarrell concluded his arguments in his book by expressing his belief that the Montanists clearly were the original "Apostolic" church. Citing Dr. Möller, Jarrell sought to prove the Montanists to be the primitive church:

> But Montanism was, nevertheless, *not a new form of Christianity;* nor were the Montanists *a new sect.* On the *contrary,* Montanism was simply a reaction of the *old,* the *primitive church,* against the obvious tendency of the day, to strike a bargain with the world and arrange herself comfortably in it.[12]

The Montanists refuted the idea that the miracles and gifts ceased in the first century. It seems strange that most Baptist historians prior to our present century acknowledge the Montanists as a part of our Baptist and evangelical heritage, while our current historians tend to deny that connection. Could it be that they are viewing both Scripture and history with the lenses of routine and tradition securely in place? By denying the supernatural work of God today, the validity of spiritual gifts, and even the powerful manifestations of the Spirit, some Baptists resist being identified with the fiery heroes of the past. Many evangelical leaders are more comfortable with the Reformers who actually persecuted our Anabaptist forebears.

TRUE TO THE END

Balthaser Hübmaier was one of those who suffered for his faith in God's supernatural workings. Born in Bavaria in 1481, he grew up to become a wise and respected scholar. He chose theology for his lifework, and upon completing his basic studies, he became vice rector at Ingolstadt and later pastored a cathedral. He was known for his pure and holy life, and a brilliant career was before him.

However, the career was less attractive to him as he realized that truth was not being upheld in many of his religious circles. In 1522, he cast his lot with the Reformers, particularly Zwingli, feeling that they were truly pursuing God's truth. One of the points of conflict in that day was the doctrine of infant baptism, and although the Reformers at first agreed that it needed to be done away with, when Hübmaier acted upon it in his Austrian church, the other Reformers—including Zwingli—withdrew from him.

He was sent a summons to appear and answer for his bold actions, but he ignored it and soon published a work entitled "Heretics and Those Who Burn Them." He took additional bold steps, abolishing the practice of Mass in the church and putting aside the priestly vestments. He encouraged his flock to know the Scriptures in their own language, to practice water baptism in the biblical way, and to know the power of the Holy Spirit on their lives.

He tried to flee to Zurich, but he was seized and imprisoned. In 1528, after being tried for heresy by the Catholic church, he was burned at the stake in the public square. His faithful wife, who supported and exhorted him to proclaim Bible truth, was drowned soon after, another martyr for Christ.[13]

You see, Baptists and other evangelicals who believe in the gifts and manifestations of the Spirit are historically legitimate in their beliefs. Ironically, perhaps we should consider some of those who are more comfortable with the formality of the Reformation as not really Baptists at all!

OTHER GROUPS

Neither time nor space permits a thorough study of other groups in church history such as the Novatians, the Donatists, the Paulicians, the Albigenses, the Patarenes, the Petrobrusians, and the Arnoldists. These are just a few of the groups who believed in New Testament power in the life of the church.

Our Anabaptist forebears were maligned for many reasons. First, they stood on the Scriptures alone as a standard for faith and practice. Second, they practiced baptism by immersion. Third, they believed in the mysteries of a personal union with Christ, dreams, visions, and supernatural gifting. Last, they supported total separation of the church from the state.

You will search in vain in Baptist history for cessationism of spiritual gifts. Granted, you may find an admission among a few of the Puritan Baptists that the gifts had waned. The spiritual deadness and coldness of their churches could explain that.

Baptists and other evangelicals should find their roots deep in the apostolic teaching of the New Testament and not in the system of man.

Even in our American history, you will find records of the persecution of Baptists or people of similar principles. Roger Williams was excommunicated by the Church of England in 1636 and fled for his life through the wild snows of New England. He established what many believe to be the first Baptist church in America in Providence, Rhode Island. Baptists in America were beaten, banished, imprisoned, and killed for the free churches they sought to establish.

Yet the Baptists of New England and Virginia secured religious freedom for America. In fact, Europeans denounced the Declaration of Independence as "an Anabaptist document."[14] Looking at the practices of Baptists in worship and revival across the years, we find much that disturbs our present complacency. There is in our history all of the accompaniment of awakening and revival including loud worship, trembling, untranslatable utterings, wild cries, falling out, and other things that seem embarrassing in today's church.

Historically, Baptists stood for a New Testament faith. This faith gave spiritual freedom to the individual Christian and to the local church where he worshiped.

When we look forward from the New Testament and see our roots in the Montanists, the Waldenses, and other fringe groups such as the Rennanites, and the Lollards among others, we find a continuation not only of baptism by immersion, but also of the power of God.

The following passage gives a clear account of some of our evangelical roots. It was taken from a speech given by John A. Broadus, a patriarch of Southern Baptists:

Shubael Stearns was born in Boston in 1706, and under the influence of the Great Awakening, attached himself, in 1745, to the Congregationalist Separates, or New Lights and began to preach. In 1751 he became a Baptist, in Connecticut, and after two or three years more, longing to carry the gospel to more destitute regions, he came, with a small colony of brethren, to Berkeley County, Va. Here he was joined by Daniel Marshall, who was of the same age with him, and had also been a Congregationalist and a Separate in Connecticut. Believing that the second coming of Christ was certainly at hand, Marshall and others sold or abandoned their property, and hastening with destitute families to the head-waters of the Susquehanna, began to labor for the conversion of the Mohawk Indians.

After eighteen months he was driven away by an Indian war, and went to Berkeley Co., Va., where, finding a Baptist Church, he examined and adopted their views about 1754. He had married, while in Connecticut, the sister of Shubael Stearns, and the two became associated in Virginia, and soon sought together a still more destitute region in North Carolina, not far from Greensboro. Here they and their little colony taught the necessity of the new birth and the consciousness of conversion, with all the excited manner and holy whine, and the nervous trembling and wild screams among their hearers, which characterized the Congregationalist Separates in Connecticut. Though at first much ridiculed, they soon had great success, building up two churches of five hundred and six hundred members. Retaining their New England name of Separates, they called themselves "Separate Baptists," and these spread rapidly into Virginia and into Georgia, though destined, when their enthusiastic excesses should have been cooled down, to be absorbed, before the end of the eighteenth century, into the body of regular Baptists.

Stearns died in North Carolina; but Marshall, ever looking out for new fields, came, after a few years, to Lexington District, in South Carolina, where he built up a church, and finally, three years before the time of which we speak, removed to Georgia, not far from Augusta, where he had already formed a considerable church. Among the unusual customs of the Separates, both Congregationalist and Baptist, was the practice of public prayer and exhortation by women; and in these exercises Marshall's wife is said to have been wonderfully impressive.[15]

Our roots lie not in the cathedrals of Europe or in the hallowed halls of academia, but in the Upper Room and later in the brush arbor. We were birthed and born along in the fire of pentecost and revival. We cannot continue to shake the hayseed of our brush arbor origin out of our hair and pretend that we are a part of some ecclesiastical hierarchy that came out of the Roman Catholic Church.

IN THE DELIVERY ROOM

At the early part of this century a revival called Azusa Street broke out in Los Angeles. The great movement of pentecostalism was birthed from that meeting. However, that wasn't the only movement. In reaction to the Azusa Street outbreak, Baptists identified with the Calvinist scholar B. B. Warfield, who wrote the first detailed argument that the gifts of the Spirit had ceased. Warfield wrote specifically to criticize the revival where the supernatural had broken forth. In addition, dispensational theology came into prominence, a doctrine that compartmentalizes Scripture and says that the age of miracles is over.

Yet many Baptists don't know that the pentecostal revival that broke out in Los Angeles in the early part of this century actually started in First Baptist Church of Los Angeles, California. The pastor, Rev. Joseph Smale, returned from a meeting with the leader of the Welsh revival, Rev. Evans Roberts. While in Wales, the Reverend Smale prayed for the same fire to fall upon his church in Los Angeles.

Day after day and night after night people waited before the Lord at that Baptist church. Revival broke out with all the manifestations and freedom witnessed across the years in awakening. Denominational walls fell, and people gathered from all across the city to experience the Lord's outpouring. A Baptist church had become the center for revival. Pastor Smale prophesied a return of apostolic gifts to the church. That was in June of 1905. The revival swept the city, and articles were written in major newspapers about the awakening.

What happened to that meeting, and why did God have to move to Azusa Street? Frank Bartleman gave his eyewitness testimony:

I went to Smale's church one night, and he resigned. The meetings had run daily in the First Baptist Church for fifteen weeks. It was now September. The officials of the church were tired of the innovation and wanted to return to the old order. He was told to either stop the revival or get out. He wisely chose the latter. But what an awful position for a church to take—to throw God out. In this same way, they later drove the Spirit of God out of the church in Wales. They tired of His presence, desiring to return to the old, cold ecclesiastical order. How blind men are! The most spiritual of Pastor Smale's members naturally followed him, with a nucleus of other workers who had gathered to him from other sources during the revival. They immediately contemplated organizing a New Testament church.[16]

Rev. Joseph Smale founded another work that thrived as the New Testament church. In that church God did a wonderful, mighty work.

Today hundreds of Baptist and evangelical churches are moving in the power of the Spirit, and awakenings are happening in every region. Yet reactionary forces rise to quench the fire of the Holy Spirit. Those affected by the work of God's Spirit are often feared and unwelcome. Baptists and others should have the freedom to operate in the Spirit within biblical parameters. Is the Baptist and evangelical tent big enough to embrace evangelical doctrines and, at the same time, welcome the Spirit's move? I pray so.

Chapter 10

UNTIDY
AWAKENINGS

$\mathcal{G}$od visits the earth in revival and renewal on a regular basis. Oddly enough, God seldom shows up where religion expects Him. Even at the coming of Jesus, God showed up in a manger, not a mansion. God has rarely poured out His Spirit upon organized religion. The reason for that is the matter of control. Religious systems tend to want to control the lives of others. But the Holy Spirit cannot be contained in man-made boxes.

God is moving in supernatural ways across the world today. These movements are usually accompanied by spiritual manifestations of every sort. There is a debate taking place over some of these accompaniments of revival. When we compare these contemporary works of God with the revivals of the past, how do they stack up?

Let's look at some examples of revival in America and see what went on. Although I don't advocate all that was recorded (in every revival there will be evidence of demonic manifestations along with the authentic move of God), it is important for us to investigate these amazing periods of breakthrough in revival history.

REVIVALS AT THE BIRTH OF THE NATION

Early America was much like our society today with religion in and morality out. The Congregational churches had what they called a halfway covenant whereby unsaved or uncommitted people could maintain positions and influence in the church.

Into that darkness came the preaching of John Wesley, George Whitefield, and Jonathan Edwards. Wesley and Whitefield shook both America and Great Britain.

JOHN WESLEY

John Wesley's meetings resulted in tens of thousands of conversions. The prolific preacher, the founder of Methodism, witnessed many strong manifestations. Let's read Wesley's accounts of these events, as written in his journal:

> Wed. 21. In the evening, such a spirit of laughter was among us, that many were much offended. But the attention of all was fixed on poor L-a-S-, whom we all knew to be no dissembler. One so violently and variously torn of the evil one did I never see before. Sometimes she laughed til almost strangled; then broke out into cursing and blaspheming; then stamped and struggled with incredible strength, so that four or five could scarce hold her: Then cried out, "O eternity, eternity! O that I had no soul! O that I had never been born!" At last she faintly called on Christ to help her. And the violence of her pangs ceased. Most of our brethren and sisters were now fully convinced, that those who were under this strange temptation could not help it.[1]

Though Wesley did not highly value manifestations, he certainly did not deny them.

We also find an account written from early in his ministry. Wesley had just expounded Acts 4, on the power of the Holy Spirit.

"We then called upon God to confirm His Word. Immediately, one that stood by (to our no small surprise) cried out aloud, with the utmost vehemence, even as the agonies of death. But we continued in prayer, till 'a new song was put in her mouth, a thanksgiving unto our God.' Soon after, two other persons (well known in this place, as laboring to live in all good conscience towards all men) were seized with strong pain, and constrained to roar for the disquietness of their heart. These also found peace." Many other wonderful cases of conviction of sin attended Wesley's preaching. It was a frequent occurrence for people to cry aloud or fall down as if dead in the meetings, so great was their anguish of heart, caused, no doubt, by the Holy Spirit convicting them of sin.[2]

It should come as no shock to us that tears and laughter are possible under the power of the Holy Spirit. Admittedly, some manifestations could be demonic as a person is becoming free, but true worship and joy can follow deliverance. Psalm 126:1–2 (NKJV) demonstrates this pattern:

When the LORD brought back the captivity of Zion,
We were like those who dream.
Then our mouth was filled with laughter,
And our tongue with singing.
Then they said among the nations,
"The LORD has done great things for them."

GEORGE WHITEFIELD

In 1740, Whitefield was twenty-six years old when he preached nearly two hundred times in a forty-five-day circuit, setting New England on fire for God. Listen to one report of the effects of his preaching:

> Mr. Whitefield had scarcely spoken for a minute on the same text when the whole auditorium could be seen to be deeply moved, to be in tears, and to be wringing hands, and the sighing, weeping, and shouting of the people could be heard. On another occasion, a German woman who could not understand English heard Whitefield preach in Philadelphia, and she was so overcome by Whitefield's gestures, expression, look, and voice, that on her return she asserted that never in her life had she had such a quickening, awakening, and edifying experience.[3]

JONATHAN EDWARDS

Jonathan Edwards's writings tell of congregations that were moved "by a mighty, invisible power" that sometimes caused "visible commotion." He recognized the inevitable problems that could arise in the midst of a move of God, and in his work "The Distinguishing Marks of a Work of the Spirit," he wrote about critics "who wait to see a work of God without difficulties and stumbling blocks that will be like the fool's waiting at the riverside to have the water all run by."[4]

Though Edwards gave cautions about Satan's desire to interpose himself in the emotion and manifestation of revival, the godly preacher certainly affirmed God-given powerful manifestations as reality. Edwards's writings report many accounts of this nature:

> The affection was quickly propagated throughout the room; many of the young people and children . . . appeared to be overcome

with the sense of the greatness and glory of divine things, and with admiration, love, joy, and praise, and compassion to others that looked upon themselves as in a state of nature (unsaved); and many others at the same time were overcome with distress about their sinful and miserable condition; so that the whole room was full of nothing but outcries, faintings, convulsions, and the like. It was pretty often so, that there were some that were so affected, and their bodies so overcome, that they could not go home, but were obliged to stay all night where they were.[5]

These revivals and others saw tens of thousands saved, and they dramatically changed the course of our nation.

REVIVALS IN THE 1800s

A study of other early American revivals reveals more of the unusual manifestations seen in the meetings of Edwards and Whitefield.

RED RIVER AWAKENING

Shortly before 1800, the Second Great Awakening broke out in America. This awakening breached all denominational lines. Isaac Backus, a noted Baptist minister, initiated a series of interdenominational prayer meetings that soon brought an awakening to New England.

Revival broke out in Kentucky in the year 1800. James McGready, a Presbyterian pastor, also held ecumenical prayer meetings for revival. He pastored three churches in an area nicknamed Rogues Harbor because of all the thieves, murderers, counterfeiters, and other criminal elements that lurked there. In a camp meeting gathering at Red River, thousands were saved. The move of God was accompanied by a mighty effusion of God's Spirit; eyewitnesses said that the ground was covered with the slain, and screams for mercy pierced the heavens.

CANE RIDGE, KENTUCKY

In 1801, a crowd of 12,500 gathered from several states for a camp meeting. Methodists, Baptists, and Presbyterians preached all over the grounds. Listen to the description of the event by Methodist circuit rider James Finley:

> The noise was like the roar of Niagara. The vast sea of human beings seemed to be agitated as if by a storm. I counted seven ministers, all preaching at one time, some on stumps, others in wagons and one standing on a tree which had, in falling, lodged against another . . .

> I stepped up on a log where I could have a better view of the surging sea of humanity. The scene that then presented itself to my mind was indescribable. At one time I saw at least five hundred swept down in a moment as if a battery of a thousand guns had been opened upon them, and then immediately followed shrieks and shouts that rent the very heavens . . .

> As to the work in general there can be no question but it is of God. The subjects of it, for the most part are deeply wounded for their sins, and can give a clear and rational account of their conversion.[6]

In my research on this revival, I was most amazed to find a book entitled *Early Tennessee Baptists* published in 1957 by the executive board of my own Tennessee Baptist Convention. The author, O. W. Taylor, took care to document the events surrounding this and subsequent great revivals. He reported in detail all the manifestations that had been recorded surrounding Cane Ridge. While he made it clear that he felt these "frantick scenes" were not proper, and noted that the Southern Baptist churches never "officially" participated in these revivals, he couldn't help pointing out an interesting fact. The Baptist churches in the area had huge increases in baptism and church membership during those days of revival![7]

CHARLES FINNEY

No one would question the effectiveness of Charles Finney, a lawyer turned evangelist. His remarkable conversion and subsequent experiences with the Holy Spirit sent him forth to preach with power.

Whitney Cross, Harvard historian, wrote a book about the Finney revivals in upper New York State and called it *The Burned Over District*. Cross believed that Finney's success in revival had much to do with the antislavery movement of the North. Finney's preaching not only won thousands, but also affected social reforms in America.[8]

Note the following excerpt from Finney's autobiography:

From Gouverneur I went to DeKalb, another village still farther north some sixteen miles. Here were a Presbyterian church and minister, but the church was small and the minister did not seem to have a very strong hold upon the people. However, I think he was decidedly a good man. I began to hold meetings in different parts of the town.

A few years previously, there had been a revival in DeKalb under the labors of the Methodists. It had been attended with a good deal of excitement, and many cases had occurred of what the Methodists call "falling under the power of God." This the

Presbyterians had resisted; consequently, a bad state of feeling had arisen between the Methodists and the Presbyterians. The Methodists accused the Presbyterians of having opposed the revival among them because of these cases of falling. As nearly as I could learn, there was a good deal of truth in this, and the Presbyterians had been decidedly in error.

I had not preached very long one evening when just at the close of my sermon, I observed a man fall from his seat near the door, and the people gathered around him to take care of him. From what I saw, I was satisfied that it was a case of falling under the power of God, as the Methodists would express it, and supposed that it was a Methodist. I must say I had a little fear that it might reproduce that state of division and alienation that had existed before. But on inquiry, I learned that it was one of the principal members of the Presbyterian church that had fallen! And it was remarkable that during this revival, there were several cases of this kind among the Presbyterians but none among the Methodists. This led to such confessions and explanation among the members of the different churches as to secure a state of great cordiality and good feeling among them.[9]

Finney saw at least 500,000 conversions in the course of his ministry. He described himself as "baptized in the Holy Spirit" and said that his own experience was accompanied by a "bellowing out" of the unutterable gushings of his heart.

PETER CARTWRIGHT

Peter Cartwright was another circuit-riding preacher who saw revival bring many thousands of converts. The power of God was evident in his meetings as well, as he recorded in his autobiography:

I have seen more than a hundred sinners fall like dead men under one powerful sermon, and I have seen and heard more than five hundred Christians all shouting aloud the high praises of God at once; and I will venture to assert that many happy thousands were awakened and converted to God at these camp meetings. Some sinners mocked, some of the old dry professors opposed, some of the old starched Presbyterian preachers preached against these exercises, but still the work went on and spread almost in every direction, gathering additional force, until our country seemed all coming home to God.[10]

Cartwright also went into detail concerning some unusual manifestations that occurred:

Just in the midst of our controversies on the subject of the powerful exercises among the people under preaching, a new exercise broke out among us, called the jerks, which was overwhelming in its effects upon the bodies and minds of the people. No matter whether they were saints or sinners, they would be taken under a warm song or sermon and seized with a convulsive jerking all over, which they could not by any possibility avoid, and the more they resisted, the more they jerked. If they would not strive against it and pray in good earnest, the jerking would usually abate. I have seen more than five hundred persons jerking at one time in my large congregations. Most usually, persons taken with the jerks, to obtain relief, as they said, would rise up and dance. Some would run, but could not get away. Some would resist; on such the jerks were generally very severe.

To see those proud young gentlemen and young ladies, dressed in their silks, jewelry, and prunella, from top to toe, take the jerks, was exciting . . . The first jerk or so, you would see their fine bonnets, caps, and combs fly; and so sudden would be the jerking of the head that their long loose hair would crack almost as loud as a wagoner's whip.[11]

Cartwright recounted yet another incident from his early years of ministry:

In 1812, a slave owner, Sister S. was struggling in agony for a clean heart. She then and there covenanted with the Lord, if He would give her the blessing, she would give up her slaves and set them free. She said this covenant had hardly been made one moment, when God filled her soul with such an overwhelming sense of Divine love, that she did not really know whether she was in or out of the body. She rose from her knees, and proclaimed to listening hundreds that she had obtained the blessing . . . She went through the vast crowd with holy shouts of joy, and exhorting all to taste and see that the Lord was gracious, and such a power attended her words that hundreds fell to the ground, and scores of souls were happily born into the kingdom of God that afternoon and during the night.[12]

These accounts concern just a few of the great waves of revival that have touched America in past years. I could recount again the story of the Los Angeles, California, revival and awakening in the early 1900s at First Baptist Church that prompted one of the most well-known awakenings in our century. It was on the other side of town that a young African-American Baptist preacher named William Seymor led a revival in the little Azusa Street mission house, assisted by Charles Parham. The movement of pentecostalism and later the charismatic movement find their roots in this revival.

All critics who throw stones across denominational lines should note that the roots of the charismatic movement today are planted in Baptist soil.

What Ties Awakenings Together

As we have looked at the history of various revivals, we note the following things are common to every awakening:

- Strong prayer emphasis
- Davidic worship (characterized by exuberant praise and bodily movement)
- Preaching of God's Word in power
- Manifestations of the Holy Spirit
- Return to holiness in living
- Breaking down of denominational, cultural, and racial walls

As we have discovered, no awakening has ever been tidy. Each major revival contained manifestations such as falling, shouting, and trembling. Across the globe, various scenes of awakening have broken out in our day that evidence unusual manifestations. Critics have jumped all over these great works. Though I have not yet personally visited the scene of God's outpouring at Brownsville Assembly of God in Florida, all reported evidence seems to verify this as a genuine move of the Holy Spirit.

At Central Baptist Church where I pastor, we have witnessed many powerful manifestations of the Spirit of God. We have seen the trembling, falling, crying, and other "untidy" events that come when the Holy Spirit touches a heart. Although we have not sought after these things, we accept them as evidences of God's move among us.

What should you seek after in a revival? While the manifestations are an evidence of God's moving, they are not what you should chase after. Instead, you should seek these lasting results that come with awakening:

1. A new commitment for the Bible

2. A new earnestness for prayer and personal devotion

3. A disgust with sin and a deep repentance

4. A fresh love and worship of Jesus

5. A loving concern for others in the body

6. A new passion for the lost

All of the incidents in this chapter were reported to you, the reader, so that you could glimpse what happened in history. Is there scriptural precedent for every manifestation? I believe there is precedent, yes, but God left a great deal open, possibly because He didn't want us to worship the method or the form of worship. In the next chapter we will look more closely at biblical precedents.

Chapter 11

MOVED BY THE SPIRIT OF GOD

*S*oon after I began to wake up to the workings of the Spirit, I was preaching to a church that had just been birthed in a north Georgia town. The pastor had resigned his previous pastorate because of objections to his stand on the validity of spiritual gifts and practices.

I had come to preach three nights. On the second night, I spoke on the need for a "harvest anointing." I called the people to be empowered to witness. I gave an altar call, and more than thirty came forward. As I began to pray, I was shocked as eleven or twelve of them "fell out," some onto their backs and some onto their faces. One man was bent over as if in pain. I had never seen such a spontaneous outpouring of God's power. Was it real?

I turned to Dr. Fred Guilbert, my minister of worship, and commented, "Would you look at them? What do you think of that!"

Suddenly, the Holy Spirit hit me in the stomach, and I involuntarily doubled over and had to take a seat. The Holy Spirit then spoke to me, warning me against judging His work in another person.

On the final night of that revival, I watched as the same people who had been so powerfully moved the night before brought the lost with them to the altars, where thirty-three souls were saved!

POWER FROM ABOVE

A fall of God's power will bring encouragement. The Bible describes these times as "times of refreshing" (Acts 3:19 NKJV). God sends a refreshing shower of spiritual life on the dry desert of our hearts. When we are burned out and want to quit, the blessed Holy Spirit shows up. Spiritual thirst brings on the refreshing shower of blessing. God promises,

> For I will pour water on him who is thirsty,
> And floods on the dry ground;
> I will pour My Spirit on your descendants,
> And My blessing on your offspring. (Isa. 44:3 NKJV)

When God's power falls, there will also be enduement. God pours out His gifts upon the church to equip it for ministry. Times of revival bring forth a fresh release of spiritual abilities to the church. Revival is a showcase of what man can do as God breaks through in His power. Acts records the first major endowment of the Holy Spirit on the disciples:

> "Cretans and Arabs—we hear them speaking in our own tongues the wonderful works of God." So they were all amazed and per-plexed, saying to one another, "Whatever could this mean?" Others mocking said, "They are full of new wine." But Peter, standing up with the eleven, raised his voice and said to them, "Men of Judea and all who dwell in Jerusalem, let this be known

to you, and heed my words. For these are not drunk, as you suppose, since it is only the third hour of the day. But this is what was spoken by the prophet Joel:

'And it shall come to pass in the last days, says God,
That I will pour out of My Spirit on all flesh;
Your sons and your daughters shall prophesy,
Your young men shall see visions,
Your old men shall dream dreams.
And on My menservants and on My maidservants
I will pour out My Spirit in those days;
And they shall prophesy.
I will show wonders in heaven above
And signs in the earth beneath:
Blood and fire and vapor of smoke.
The sun shall be turned into darkness,
And the moon into blood,
Before the coming of the great and awesome day of the LORD.
And it shall come to pass
That whoever calls on the name of the LORD
Shall be saved.'" (Acts 2:11–21 NKJV)

In addition, when God shows up, there will be a special enduement on a person. Jesus promised, "Behold, I send the Promise of My Father upon you; but tarry in the city of Jerusalem until you are endued with power from on high" (Luke 24:49 NKJV).

The word *endue* actually means "to clothe." This has to do with the visible work of the Holy Spirit. Just as you can see clothing on an individual's body, so is enduement the tangible evidence that God has come upon a person's spirit.

The late Dr. Martyn Lloyd-Jones, perhaps the greatest expositor of Scripture in this century, believed that the "sealing of the Holy Spirit" was no less than an overwhelming experience by which God touches a believer and brings that believer to full assurance. He believed that the Holy Spirit comes upon a believer and gives him a foretaste of heaven. Enduement is like a down payment of the power of the world to come.[1]

How does the Holy Spirit manifest Himself? In other chapters, we studied some of the gifts, such as tongues, and the phenomenon of falling. Let us now look at a few other manifestations whereby the Spirit shows Himself.

SHAKING OR TREMBLING

Trembling has been a regular occurrence in many services of our church. Trembling can be mild or convulsive. God's Word includes numerous incidents where people trembled under God's power. Often the trembling was a result of fear in His presence.

> "Do you not fear Me?" says the LORD.
> "Will you not tremble at My presence,
> Who have placed the sand as the bound of the sea,
> By a perpetual decree, that it cannot pass beyond it?
> And though its waves toss to and fro,
> Yet they cannot prevail;
> Though they roar, yet they cannot pass over it." (Jer. 5:22 NKJV)

And he said to me, "O Daniel, man greatly beloved, understand the words that I speak to you, and stand upright, for I have now been sent to you." While he was speaking this word to me, I stood trembling. Then he said to me, "Do not fear, Daniel, for from the first day that you set your heart to understand, and to humble yourself before your God, your words were heard; and I have come because of your words." (Dan. 10:11–12 NKJV)

When I heard, my body trembled;
My lips quivered at the voice;
Rottenness entered my bones;
And I trembled in myself,
That I might rest in the day of trouble. (Hab. 3:16 NKJV)

Other times, trembling occurred when someone was delivered or healed. In Mark 5:33 (NKJV), we find that the woman healed of the issue of blood "fearing and trembling, knowing what had happened to her, came and fell down before Him and told Him the whole truth."

In addition, individuals were known to tremble under conviction or at their conversion. In Paul's day, Governor Felix felt the convicting power of the Holy Spirit, as recorded in Acts 24:25 (KJV): "And as he reasoned of righteousness, temperance, and judgment to come, Felix trembled, and answered, Go thy way for this time; when I have a convenient season, I will call for thee." Acts 9:6 (NKJV) records Paul's conversion when he, "trembling and astonished," asked God for new direction.

Every incident of the Spirit's filling in the New Testament does not indicate trembling but, it certainly is possible. In Acts 4:31, the entire room was shaken as the apostles received the baptism of the Holy Spirit.

Trembling was common during the Great Awakening and is certainly a legitimate expression of the conviction of the Holy Spirit. This manifestation gave the early American Quakers their name. Rev. Barton Stone, a leader of the Cane Ridge revival, told in his 1847 autobiography of the many bodily "exercises" he witnessed at frontier revivals:

Sometimes the subject of "the jerks" would be affected in some one member of the body, and sometimes in the whole system. When the head alone was affected, it would be jerked backward and forward, or from side to side, so quickly that the features of the face could not be distinguished. When the whole system was affected, I have seen the person stand in one place, and jerk backward and forward in quick succession, their head nearly touching the floor behind and before.[2]

A young man who serves as a musician in our church wrote out his testimony concerning his experiences of this nature:

During a Sunday morning service, God prompted me to raise my hands during a particular worship chorus. Normally, I wouldn't argue with Him, but I didn't really like the song this time! His Spirit kept insisting, and so I obeyed. When I did, my hands began to shake. It was a wonderful feeling! After a couple of other choruses, the shaking stopped. As I reflected on the experience, I recalled that early in the service, I had asked God to touch me in a special way. These "kisses from the Father" have a way of releasing me from any pride, and taking me out of my comfort zone. He has a way of coming out of that little box I try to put Him in and showing Himself to be more awesome than I ever imagined.

JOY AND SINGING

Every so often, holy laughter and an outbreak of joy accompany a movement of the Holy Spirit. Two Scriptures immediately come to mind when I think of the joy surrounding the work of God:

Then was our mouth filled with laughter, and our tongue with singing: then said they among the heathen, The LORD hath done great things for them. (Ps. 126:2 KJV)

A time to weep,
> And a time to laugh;
A time to mourn,
> And a time to dance. (Eccl. 3:4 NKJV)

Although these verses don't instruct us specifically in the use of laughter by the Holy Spirit, you can't get away from the fact that freedom from the bondage of the enemy produces real joy. Salvation is a *rescue!* What happened to the Israelites in the natural often can be applied to the spiritual realm. First Corinthians 10:11 (NKJV) indicates that they are "as examples" to us. The joy resulting from freedom may lead to a continuing desire to sing and to praise Jesus. Simon Peter knew this truth when he wrote,

In this you greatly rejoice, though now for a little while, if need be, you have been grieved by various trials, that the genuineness of your faith, being much more precious than gold that perishes, though it is tested by fire, may be found to praise, honor, and glory at the revelation of Jesus Christ, whom having not seen you love. Though now you do not see Him, yet believing, you rejoice with joy inexpressible and full of glory. (1 Peter 1:6–8 NKJV)

Jonathan Edwards, in his book *Religious Affections,* told of many instances during his meetings when people would burst into laughter, and moments later be melted into tears when the Spirit fell.[3]

In many revivals, this joy would express itself in singing. An example comes from the testimony of George Whitefield:

> Soon after this I found and felt in myself that I was delivered from the burden that had so heavily oppressed me; the spirit of mourning was taken from me and I knew what it was truly to rejoice in God my Saviour, and for some time could not avoid singing psalms wherever I was. But my joy gradually became more settled and, blessed be God, has abode and increased in my soul, saving a few casual intermissions, ever since. Thus were the days of my mourning ended.[4]

Again, we read Reverend Stone's account of the beautiful singing of people touched by the Spirit in his day:

> This singing exercise is more unaccountable than anything else I ever saw. The subject in a very happy state of mind would sing most melodiously, not from the mouth or nose, but entirely in the breast, the sounds issuing thence. Such music silenced everything, and attracted the attention of all. It was most heavenly. None could ever be tired of hearing it.[5]

DRUNKENNESS OR EUPHORIA

On the day of pentecost, an accusation leveled against the apostles was drunkenness. Look at these verses once more:

> Others mocking said, "They are full of new wine." But Peter, standing up with the eleven, raised his voice and said to them, "Men of Judea and all who dwell in Jerusalem, let this be known to you, and

heed my words. For these are not drunk, as you suppose, since it is only the third hour of the day." (Acts 2:13–15 NKJV)

Notice also the words of Jeremiah:

> My heart within me is broken
> Because of the prophets;
> All my bones shake.
> I am like a drunken man,
> And like a man whom wine has overcome,
> Because of the LORD,
> And because of His holy words. (Jer. 23:9 NKJV)

Paul later taught that it was possible to be drunk on the Holy Spirit. Just as some men fill up their bellies with wine and become powered by the influence, so can the believer become powered by the fullness of the Spirit.

> Do not be drunk with wine, in which is dissipation; but be filled with the Spirit, speaking to one another in psalms and hymns and spiritual songs, singing and making melody in your heart to the Lord, giving thanks always for all things to God the Father in the name of our Lord Jesus Christ, submitting to one another in the fear of God. (Eph. 5:18–21 NKJV)

This verse is not a contrast, but a comparison. Being filled with the Spirit may cause you to do some things you may not usually do. Some people experience a sense of dizziness or euphoria when they experience this filling. While these manifestations may occur, more important, the Holy Spirit will create in you a fresh hunger for

Scripture, a new love for Jesus, and a new display of the fruit of the Spirit in your life.

CRYING AND WEEPING

Hardly anyone would question the validity of tears as a spiritual reflection of God's move. God cherishes the tears of His people. David recorded his prayer,

You number my wanderings;
Put my tears into Your bottle;
Are they not in Your book? (Ps. 56:8 NKJV)

One may also *seek* the Lord with tears:

My tears have been my food day and night,
While they continually say to me,
"Where is your God?" (Ps. 42:3 NKJV)

Repentance and concern bring tears. When revival broke out under Nehemiah, there was much loud weeping:

Nehemiah, who was the governor, Ezra the priest and scribe, and
the Levites who taught the people said to all the people, "This day
is holy to the LORD your God; do not mourn nor weep." For all
the people wept, when they heard the words of the Law. (Neh. 8:9
NKJV)

It is comforting to know that God is responsive to our weeping, as we see in 2 Chronicles 34:27 (NKJV):

"Because your heart was tender, and you humbled yourself before God when you heard His words against this place and against its inhabitants, and you humbled yourself before Me, and you tore your clothes and wept before Me, I also have heard you," says the LORD.

Jeremiah wept over the spiritual condition of Israel:

Oh, that my head were waters,
And my eyes a fountain of tears,
That I might weep day and night
For the slain of the daughter of my people! (Jer. 9:1 NKJV)

Jesus Christ wept publicly and unashamedly. On one occasion, a woman who had been of questionable reputation wept over His feet and dried them with her hair (Luke 7:38). The apostle Paul wept with the Ephesian elders as he left their city. He reminded them of his ministry of tears during the time that he served with them.

Perhaps the most telling scriptural example of tears in the church is the parable of the sinner's prayer found in Luke 18. Remember that the synagogue was the forerunner of the early church, and it was a place of expression. A Pharisee and a tax collector went into the synagogue to pray. The Pharisee spoke forth a glittering prayer that was filled with pride, but the tax collector beat upon his breast and cried, "God, be merciful to me a sinner!" (Luke 18:13 NKJV). Jesus commented that the tax collector was justified because of his humility.

We need more of that kind of humility in our churches today. Loud weeping may often be a part of true revival. We are seeing it today when God breaks through.

DANCING AND BODILY MOVEMENTS

The word *praise* is often tied to the Hebrew word for *dance,* which means "to whirl around." King David was known to dance before the Lord with all his might (2 Sam. 6:14). People may be observed jumping, running, and moving under the power of the Holy Spirit.

Again, Scripture does not specify this is an activity found often in the church, but there is precedent for such happenings. When God touched the disabled legs of the beggar at the temple, the Bible tells us that Peter pulled the man to his feet: "So he, leaping up, stood and walked and entered the temple with them—walking, leaping, and praising God. And all the people saw him walking and praising God" (Acts 3:8–9 NKJV).

We should be careful not to hastily dismiss such bodily manifestations. We cannot always know what circumstances surround the leaping and jumping!

PURPOSES FOR MANIFESTATIONS

Manifestations are often responses to the Lord's presence. At other times, God uses manifestations to break our pride. Our flesh does not want to be humbled or exposed before others. God can also use the unusual happenings to expose religious traditionalism and its bondage. God may offend the flesh in order to expose a proud heart.

In some instances, God's plan may be to declare the sovereignty of His Holy Spirit through supernatural manifestations. Jesus warned Nicodemus that the Holy Spirit cannot be contained or controlled by the flesh. God desires for us to be continuously filled with the Holy Spirit. It pleases Him to bring upon us fresh anointings and revelation of His presence.

I was at a recent staff retreat sitting on the front row with my wife while a guest pastor ministered to all of us. The Spirit of God came upon me, and I fell over on my wife and then to the floor. I felt sharp pain intermittently in the area of my stomach. As I lay there, God spoke and said, "This is the firstfruits of revival; I will pour out My Spirit on the church." When I got up, I turned in the Bible to Romans 8:21–23 (NKJV):

> Because the creation itself also will be delivered from the bondage of corruption into the glorious liberty of the children of God. For we know that the whole creation groans and labors with birth pangs together until now. Not only that, but we also who have the firstfruits of the Spirit, even we ourselves groan within ourselves, eagerly waiting for the adoption, the redemption of our body.

The groaning in me was the deep desire and sense that God's purpose was to be fulfilled in our church.

HOW CAN WE BE SURE THESE THINGS ARE REAL?

As you see manifestations, you know that they must be coming from somewhere. Unfortunately, they sometimes are a person's own emotional response. On some occasions, they may even be demonic. Other times, people may be imitating one another. But you always must consider that what you see could be a genuine work of the Holy Spirit.

The truth is, you cannot always know. As human beings, we cannot unfailingly discern the spiritual condition of another heart. It is true that in every revival through the ages, manifestations have occurred that were strictly emotional acts and demonic imitations.

Why would Satan counterfeit these experiences? Consider this: counterfeiters always make copies of something valuable! Satan loves to counterfeit true biblical experiences in order to discredit the work of God. Second Corinthians 11:14 (NKJV) warns us, "Satan himself transforms himself into an angel of light."

Even though we cannot know for sure, we can test the manifestations in the following ways.

1. THE WORD TEST

Ask, Does what we see have biblical precedence? What principles of Scripture support these actions? The early Christians knew the importance of this: "These were more fair-minded than those in Thessalonica, in that they received the word with all readiness, and searched the Scriptures daily to find out whether these things were so" (Acts 17:11 NKJV).

2. THE WARFARE TEST

The church should test the Spirit in a person:

> Beloved, do not believe every spirit, but test the spirits, whether they are of God; because many false prophets have gone out into the world. By this you know the Spirit of God: Every spirit that confesses that Jesus Christ has come in the flesh is of God, and every spirit that does not confess that Jesus Christ has come in the flesh is not of God. And this is the spirit of the Antichrist, which you have heard was coming, and is now already in the world. (1 John 4:1–3 NKJV)

Leaders should ask the persons in whom there is a tongue, a sign, or a manifestation to confess by the Spirit controlling them that Jesus is Lord. If they cannot, then they likely are trafficking with a demon.

Pastors and leaders must exercise discernment and rebuke those who are not of the Spirit.

3. THE WORKS TEST

What has the manifestation or sign done for the believer or for the church? Has the sign or manifestation become an end unto itself? The signs are never the destination. The real test of the Spirit's work will be clearly displayed in a deeper love for Jesus, a new hunger for Scripture, a passion for lost souls, a thirst for righteousness, and a new love for others.

WHAT IS DIVINE ORDER?

In 1 Corinthians 14:40 (NKJV), we read, "Let all things be done decently and in order." God's order may not be our order. Our lives are so out of order that we need to be certain that we are able to judge properly what *is* order. What God has decreed as order may not be what we consider comfortable. Our ideas of order may be nothing less than weak attempts to control our own spiritual lives, unconsciously leaving God out of the loop.

In 1 Chronicles 13 when David was bringing up the ark to Jerusalem, he failed to do it according to God's instructions. Consequently, a man was killed. Later in 1 Chronicles 15:13 (NKJV), David was careful to observe the correct "order": "For because you did not do it the first time, the LORD our God broke out against us, because we did not consult Him about the proper order."

When David practiced obedience, the outcome was dramatically different. God's order didn't restrict his expression in worship, for a mass choir, an orchestra, sacrifices, shouting, and dancing before the Lord accompanied the ark. That was massive freedom!

David knew that he was to love God with all his heart, soul, mind, and strength, but that time, in obedience to the accompanying instructions.

God continues to expect us to obey and to heed His order. Acts 5 tells the tragic story of a couple who lied to the Holy Spirit, not fulfilling their responsibility in giving to God. Ananias and Sapphira pretended they were on the right track; they at least brought a portion of their tithe to the church, but in holding back an amount, they were out of order, and death was the result.

Let us not ignore the instructions of God and the prompting of the Holy Spirit as we seek to exercise His gifts and function in the church. It is all about obedience.

PROPER RESPONSES TO MANIFESTATIONS

As you examine manifestations in the church, it is important to ask searching questions:

- Is God leading your leaders? If so, then trust your spiritual leaders and open your heart to God.

- Are you afraid of what you don't understand? Just because you don't understand it does not mean it's not of God.

- Are you causing problems by your own stand on these issues? These things can become divisive. Be sure that you are not divisive. Don't expect everyone to accept your experience or to repeat it. If you have not expressed certain manifestations, don't judge others who have. Let God be God!

- Are you open to what God may be doing in others? Even if you don't agree, love them.

What you receive from God will always be good for you and the church. Remember what Jesus said,

> I say to you, ask, and it will be given to you; seek, and you will find; knock, and it will be opened to you. For everyone who asks receives, and he who seeks finds, and to him who knocks it will be opened. If a son asks for bread from any father among you, will he give him a stone? Or if he asks for a fish, will he give him a serpent instead of a fish? Or if he asks for an egg, will he offer him a scorpion? If you then, being evil, know how to give good gifts to your children, how much more will your heavenly Father give the Holy Spirit to those who ask Him! (Luke 11:9–13 NKJV)

God will give you good gifts to bless you and the kingdom!

Part 4

A RENEWED CHURCH

Chapter 12

DANCING WITH DAVID

I'll never forget the Sunday that our church learned yet another lesson about the power of praise and worship. The Sunday worship service was well under way, and the congregation was especially exuberant in singing and praise. Many hands were lifted, and tears of joy were evident on the faces of some worshipers.

From my vantage point on the platform, I saw the young man step out into an aisle and make his way forward to the altar. He stood quietly, looking up at me expectantly. At first I thought he might be an usher who was slightly premature in getting to his place for the offering time. However, as I stepped down and took his hand, he said, "I need to be saved now."

I had not yet spoken a word of my sermon, read any Scripture, or given an invitation, and yet something welled up within the man as the praises of God's people lifted toward heaven. He couldn't wait another moment, and he stepped out under conviction from the Holy Spirit. We joyfully led the man to Christ, and taking the Holy Spirit's cue, we opened the altar for any others who needed to make a decision.

Over the past few years, there have been times in the services of our church where God has stepped in during the music and worship, making it necessary to throw our order of service to the floor as the Holy Spirit ministered to people. My sermon outline has stayed tucked away in my Bible many times as God chose to minister through the praise and worship music.

Some people believe that God can do His saving work only through preaching and "sermonizing." I have heard of churches that do not let any service close without a sermon from the pulpit. Do not misunderstand—I firmly believe that God has ordained "the foolishness of preaching" as a main tool for touching lives. However, the church that downplays the important role of music in worship and praise is likely quenching the Holy Spirit's work in the body.

JUST A PASSING FAD?

The path to renewal in praise and worship came in small steps at our church. We had hosted Jack Taylor, a noted teacher of the deeper life, for the conference "The Hallelujah Factor," a study on praise and worship in the church. I sensed God had something to teach us.

It was shortly after my encounter with the Holy Spirit, and while still dealing with the aftershocks of the scandal that surrounded our former music/youth minister, that we asked Frank Steil, a layman in the church, to step forward as interim worship leader. Frank began to teach the congregation fresh new choruses and encouraged more freedom in worship.

I thought the choruses and the hand-clapping rhythms were just a fad, but soon I realized there was much more behind the new worship style.

Meanwhile, our search for a music minister continued, and God had been working on someone on the other side of the country to fill our need. Dr. Fred Guilbert had been raised in a rather conservative church, but ever since he was a young person, he had felt there was something missing in the church house. He would hear preachers expound on the glorious praise told about in the book of Revelation, and he would wonder, "Why don't we sing like that now? Shouldn't we be rehearsing here on earth for what we will do in heaven?"

God moved this precious brother into our church as we were just getting our feet planted into the true spirit of worship. Although some people resisted the new style of worship, we soon saw spontaneity and freshness fill the services.

A true turning point came after a Promise Keepers event in 1995. Nearly two hundred of our men had driven from Tennessee to Indiana for the rally. Men were powerfully changed and affected by the meeting. They were so excited about their life-changing experiences that they decided to drive through the night on Saturday so they could share their excitement with the church.

The travel-weary men filled the choir loft that Sunday, and as they began to sing out the songs that they had learned at Promise Keepers, the women and children in the audience began to weep. There was electricity in the air, a true excitement to be worshiping at the feet of Jesus! That holy fire continues to this day in our services.

Today, many evangelical churches are experiencing this type of renewal. Part of that move of God is a resurgence of praise and worship marked by a liberty of expression. Critics label this style of music "charismatic," "pentecostal," or a "church growth fad." Others say that it is pure worldliness, and that it is disturbance. This movement has often pitted the traditional, the ritual, and the formal against the exuberant freedom given by God. I believe that this return to praise and worship is biblical and an actual fulfillment of prophecy.

THE TABERNACLE OF DAVID

An interesting pair of prophecies can be found in both the Old Testament and the New Testament. A casual look at the two prophecies may cause us to miss their deep significance. All of us know about the tabernacle that Moses established (Ex. 36–40), but very few of us know about the tabernacle that David built to restore worship and praise in Jerusalem. The story of these events is found in 1 Chronicles 13–16. In these chapters, David expressed his desire to move the ark of the covenant from the old tabernacle of Moses in Gibeon to the new capital city of Jerusalem. David encountered many difficulties and pitfalls as he tried to restore worship to the nation.

The tabernacle of David differed from the tabernacle of Moses in that there was no veil. The ark was accessible to all. The glory of the Lord revealed in the shekinah glory cloud was obvious to all who came near. Amos 9 further speaks of Israel's return and restoration to their land. Here is the prophecy of a restoration that is obviously directed to the future church age:

> "On that day I will raise up
> The tabernacle of David, which has fallen down,
> And repair its damages;
> I will raise up its ruins,
> And rebuild it as in the days of old;

That they may possess the remnant of Edom,
And all the Gentiles who are called by My name,"
Says the LORD who does this thing. (Amos 9:11–12 NKJV)

Acts 15 cites the restoration of David's tabernacle as a prophecy for the gentile church:

After this I will return
And will rebuild the tabernacle of David, which has fallen down;
I will rebuild its ruins,
And I will set it up;
So that the rest of mankind may seek the LORD,
Even all the Gentiles who are called by My name,
Says the LORD who does all these things. (Acts 15:16–17 NKJV)

This prophecy is not a call to pitch an actual tent, but a call to restore Davidic worship. While this prophecy was partially fulfilled when the gospel reached the Gentiles, it still remains to be completed. The New Testament church in the last days is to experience significant restoration of praise and worship. The church is to discover that there is no veil hanging between her and the Lord Jesus! We can enter and enjoy His presence.

The style of worship you see, hear, and experience in many progressive churches may be somewhat different from what you are used to. Some ask the question, "Is this wrong because it is different?" The answer obviously is no. Powerful worship is found in formal church atmospheres as well. The better questions to ask should be, "Is this biblical? Is God in this place? What are the motives of the hearts?"

First Chronicles 15:1–29 describes the joyous return of the ark

(God's presence) to Jerusalem and David's tabernacle. As we await the Lord's coming, this same type of sacrifice and celebration can mark our worship. God loves to stretch us beyond where we are.

BIBLICAL PRINCIPLES REGARDING PRAISE AND WORSHIP

When we come to praise God, we can learn from David some of the elements of true praise. However, we need to make some preliminary observations.

In evangelical Christianity there are presently two styles of worship. There is the liturgical style that is very formal, following a set order. It is usually quiet and dignified and includes written prayers and responses. Those of this tradition are often uncomfortable in the second style we call "the free church style." Both styles have defenders and detractors.

I firmly believe that some of the practices demonstrated by both groups are not represented in Scripture. A lukewarm order of service that creates a predictable response can be dead and lifeless. However, a performance-oriented worship, focused on the goal to entertain rather than to experience Christ's presence, is just as lifeless in its core.

Celebration may or may not be formal, but it should be skillful and orderly. Celebration should not be misunderstood as confusion: "God is not the author of confusion" (1 Cor. 14:33 NKJV).

The principles for true praise are outlined in the Scriptures.

WE SHOULD WORSHIP CHRIST CONTINUALLY

Is worship confined to services? No! God is uplifted by our personal praise.

Let all those who seek You rejoice and be glad in You;
And let those who love Your salvation say continually,
"Let God be magnified!" (Ps. 70:4 NKJV)

Therefore by Him let us continually offer the sacrifice of praise to God, that is, the fruit of our lips, giving thanks to His name. (Heb. 13:15 NKJV)

WE SHOULD WORSHIP CHRIST IN CHURCH

When the body of Christ gathers together, worship should be the primary focus. Worship is an expression of our love for God.

I will declare Your name to My brethren;
In the midst of the assembly I will praise You. (Ps. 22:22 NKJV)

I will give You thanks in the great assembly;
I will praise You among many people. (Ps. 35:18 NKJV)

I will declare Your name to My brethren;
In the midst of the assembly I will sing praise to You. (Heb. 2:12 NKJV)

WE SHOULD WORSHIP CHRIST WITH THE LOST PRESENT

Elements of worship have a drawing effect; they are attractive to the lost soul.

He has put a new song in my mouth—
Praise to our God;
Many will see it and fear,
And will trust in the LORD. (Ps. 40:3 NKJV)

WE SHOULD WORSHIP GOD SO THAT PRAISE CAN BE HEARD

It is perfectly in order to worship audibly; in fact, Scripture mandates it.

Oh, bless our God, you peoples!
And make the voice of His praise to be heard. (Ps. 66:8 NKJV)

These sounds of worship could include the following:

- Shouting: "Let Your saints shout for joy" (Ps. 132:9 NKJV).

- Singing: "And do not be drunk with wine, in which is dissipation; but be filled with the Spirit, speaking to one another in psalms and hymns and spiritual songs, singing and making melody in your heart to the Lord, giving thanks always for all things to God the Father in the name of our Lord Jesus Christ" (Eph. 5:18–20 NKJV).

- Laughter: We are free to follow the worship patterns of the psalms: "Then our mouth was filled with laughter, and our tongue with singing" (Ps. 126:2 NKJV).

- Musical instruments: "Play skillfully with a loud noise" (Ps. 33:3 KJV).

- Clapping: "Oh, clap your hands, all you peoples! Shout to God with the voice of triumph!" (Ps. 47:1 NKJV).

- Children: When Jesus was questioned about the children praising Him in the streets as He arrived in Jerusalem, Jesus reminded them of a verse in David's psalm, "Have you never read, 'Out of the mouth of babes and nursing infants You have perfected praise'?" (Matt. 21:16 NKJV).

WE SHOULD WORSHIP GOD WITH OUR BODIES

David used his body to express his love to the Lord. There is a place for physical expression in worship. How should we use the body in worship? "Present your bodies a living sacrifice" (Rom. 12:1 NKJV). Sometimes that may mean moving out of our comfort zones and allowing our love for God to be revealed outwardly.

WE CAN LIFT UP OUR HANDS

Both the Old and New Testaments indicate that lifting up of the hands can be part of worship.

> Thus I will bless You while I live;
> I will lift up my hands in Your name. (Ps. 63:4 NKJV)

> I desire therefore that the men pray everywhere, lifting up holy
> hands, without wrath and doubting. (1 Tim. 2:8 NKJV)

WE SHOULD WORSHIP GOD WITH THE SOUL AND SPIRIT

You are body—world conscious. And you are soul—self-conscious: "Bless the LORD, O my soul" (Ps. 103:1 NKJV). In addition, you are spirit—God conscious. When you are saved, your spirit comes alive in Jesus Christ. Praise is the exercise of the Spirit. Praise brings strength to your spirit, which worships "God in the Spirit" (Phil. 3:3 NKJV). Mary praised God by saying, "My spirit has rejoiced in God my Savior" (Luke 1:47 NKJV).

WE SHOULD WORSHIP ACCORDING TO THE WORD OF GOD

Everything David did in worship was from the Word of God: "In God (I will praise His word)" (Ps. 56:4, 10 NKJV).

WHAT DO PRAISE AND WORSHIP ACCOMPLISH?

Praise is pleasing to God. God's number one requirement was given in Matthew 22:37–38 (NKJV), "'You shall love the LORD your God with all your heart, with all your soul, and with all your mind.' This is the first and great commandment." He enjoys hearing His saints praise His name.

Praise also brings joy to the believer's heart. Praise in your life replaces heaviness and sorrow. As he prophesied about the coming ministry of Jesus, Isaiah wrote of the changes that would occur as Jesus touched lives:

> To console those who mourn in Zion,
> To give them beauty for ashes,
> The oil of joy for mourning,
> The garment of praise for the spirit of heaviness;
> That they may be called trees of righteousness,
> The planting of the LORD, that He may be glorified. (Isa. 61:3 NKJV)

Incidentally, this verse proves that praise must be outwardly manifested. As Isaiah described the change from heaviness to joy, he used the phrase "garment of praise." Christians who resist practicing exuberance in worship, saying, "I'm praising God in my heart," should note that a garment is *external*. When was the last time you put clothing on your insides?

Praise is an expression of our love for God. When worship is mentioned in the Bible, it is connected with intimacy. It is our "love talk" with our Savior.

I also feel that Scripture indicates that when we praise God, He releases spiritual forces to bind the enemies of His people. Praise and warfare often go hand in hand throughout Scripture. Psalm 149:5–9 (NKJV) tells of the exciting result of high praise:

> Let the saints be joyful in glory;
> Let them sing aloud on their beds.
> Let the high praises of God be in their mouth,
> And a two-edged sword in their hand,
> To execute vengeance on the nations,
> And punishments on the peoples;
> To bind their kings with chains,
> And their nobles with fetters of iron;
> To execute on them the written judgment—
> This honor have all His saints.
> Praise the LORD!

Praise is a powerful weapon! Perhaps one of the most interesting biblical accounts of this is found in 2 Chronicles 20. Jehoshaphat, as leader of Judah, discovered that the mighty armies of Moab and Ammon were almost upon them. He was greatly afraid and called the people to a fast. The entire nation, including small children, showed up for a prayer service where Jehoshaphat begged God to reveal Himself as faithful once more to the nation. As the prayer came to an end, one of the singers spoke up and prophesied:

> Then the Spirit of the LORD came upon Jahaziel the son of Zechariah, the son of Benaiah, the son of Jeiel, the son of Mattaniah, a Levite of the sons of Asaph, in the midst of the assembly. And he said, "Listen, all you of Judah and you inhabitants of Jerusalem, and you, King Jehoshaphat! Thus says the LORD to you: 'Do not be afraid nor dismayed because of this great multitude, for

the battle is not yours, but God's. Tomorrow go down against them. They will surely come up by the Ascent of Ziz, and you will find them at the end of the brook before the Wilderness of Jeruel. You will not need to fight in this battle. Position yourselves, stand still and see the salvation of the LORD, who is with you, O Judah and Jerusalem!' Do not fear or be dismayed; tomorrow go out against them, for the LORD is with you." And Jehoshaphat bowed his head with his face to the ground, and all Judah and the inhabitants of Jerusalem bowed before the LORD, worshiping the LORD. Then the Levites of the children of the Kohathites and of the children of the Korahites stood up to praise the LORD God of Israel with voices loud and high. (2 Chron. 20:14–19 NKJV)

After the singer had finished his prophecy, the choir began to sing. Of course, they still had to deal with the enemy, but Jehoshaphat's battle plan was soon ready.

And when he had consulted with the people, he appointed those who should sing to the LORD, and who should praise the beauty of holiness, as they went out before the army and were saying:

"Praise the Lord,
For His mercy endures forever."

Now when they began to sing and to praise, the LORD set ambushes against the people of Ammon, Moab, and Mount Seir, who had come against Judah; and they were defeated. (2 Chron. 20:21–22 NKJV)

Your battles can be won through your praise and worship of God!

Jesus Himself helped to strengthen and prepare His disciples at the Last Supper by leading them in a hymn as they closed their Passover meal. He knew what lay ahead for them, and He knew they needed a song to face the coming days.

Praise literally brings God on the scene, for Scripture says that God inhabits the praise of His people (Ps. 22:3). Though God is always resident in the life of a believer as He promised, His presence and power seem to be released as a flood in an atmosphere of praise.

Praise also prepares the heart to hear the Word of God, clearing the mind. As a young man, David played for King Saul when he was troubled and oppressed, and it soothed the ruler's spirit. You may find that as you praise the Lord in the midst of problems and confusion, your mind will become clearer, and your decisions will be easier to make.

In addition, worship is a mark of the Holy Spirit's filling and often the very first sign of His visitation. It is spiritual conversation, allowing communication with Him and a way to join with others in expressions of love to God, as the Scripture says, "singing and making melody in your heart to the Lord" (Eph. 5:19 NKJV).

THE RESULT OF ABSENT PRAISE

Many argue against the idea of David's tabernacle being established today. A popular argument is one of semantics—they claim that the word used for "tabernacle" in the promises of the restoration of David's tabernacle refers only to the future establishment of his kingly line rather than the setting up of a fresh and exuberant place of worship. They claim this promise will be fulfilled in the Millennium when David's line will once again reign on earth. However, a careful study reveals that the words used to discuss both Moses' and David's tabernacles are the same, and that the word represents a literal "house of worship."

In 1 Chronicles 15:29, we cannot help observing Michal, David's wife, as a sad picture of the church that despises praise. Michal represents the believers who are afraid to praise God as well as the believers who look down on the individuals who praise Him unashamedly. Michal typifies the church that refuses to praise. Look at her likeness to the church:

- Like the church, she was a king's daughter.

- Like the church, she was purchased with the price of blood (David slew two hundred Philistines to win her as his bride).

- Like the church, she was a bride of the king.

- Like the church, she had once had a love relationship with her king and bridegroom.

David's love for her was so great that he refused to be crowned king until she was restored to him. But Michal had forsaken her beloved. Like the church in Revelation 2:1–10, she had left her first love. Until the day of her death she was called Saul's daughter rather than David's bride. She maintained her identity with the old regime and the old way of life.

How closely this tragic account reflects those today who despise and mock the emotional praise and worship environments. Could it be possible that some congregations are slowly dying because they know that they should put the focus of their services back on Christ, and yet they stand afraid to open themselves up to any change in the way they worship?

The curse on Michal for not praising God was a loss of intimacy with her beloved. Second Samuel 6:23 (NKJV) tells this sad truth: "Therefore Michal the daughter of Saul had no children to the day of her death." If a church despises praise, the curse of barrenness in true conversions to Christ will come upon it. Real growth will cease as the intimate relationship with Christ is lost.

My prayer is that you will be open to the Spirit of God. Let God set you free to lift up your heart, your voice, your hands, and your life as a sacrifice of praise to Him, for He is worthy of all you can offer.

Chapter 13

STORMING THE GATES
OF HELL

In the summer of 1968, I was at a youth camp in the mountains near Birmingham, Alabama. It was a glorious night for me, a twenty-one-year-old pastor. My wife of less than a year had been gloriously saved. Though she had been faithful to the church all her life, she had never experienced the new birth.

After she had left to get her group of girls into their beds, I went along with some other pastors to pray. I shouted, laughed, and cried over the wonderful events of the evening. The others rejoiced with me. Suddenly, a young man came toward us, groaning and saying, "I can't get it out. It won't leave me alone." I stood by helplessly while another minister cast out a demonic force. The boy collapsed to the ground. When he got up, he was led to Christ, and his life was gloriously changed.

He went home from that camp, and at a testimony time at the First Baptist Church, he shared what had happened. Very few were happy about it! All of us pastors and leaders who had led the youth camp were taken aside and strongly put in our place. I remember one of my older deacons warning me about the dangers of Holy Roller religion.

In response to the objections those leaders had years ago, I have to say that today that delivered boy is forty-five years old and is powerfully serving the Lord.

At that summer camp, I had my first glimpse of the invisible war. It seemed too unreal and too overwhelming, so I pushed it out of my mind until one morning in 1981. I was in the first year of my current pastorate. I came into my office that day to find a young high school girl in distress. She explained she had experienced a gruesome nightmare. It had tormented the girl. Even in my ignorance, my spirit flew back in time, and I recognized the same forces I had witnessed thirteen years earlier at that summer camp.

As best as I knew how, I took authority and cast down the strongholds and rebuked the tormenting spirits. The Lord was faithful to me even in my ignorance, and the girl was wonderfully set free. That young woman is an effective, Spirit-filled Christian today.

It wasn't until after my spiritual awakening in 1989 that I really woke up to the spiritual battle that Christians face. I slowly discovered that demon possession and demon oppression are as real today as they were in the first century. Through prayer meetings I attended, special speakers invited to my church, and the wonderful counseling tools developed by Neil Anderson, I learned to be battle ready against the enemy. Between 1989 and 1992, I had more than one hundred confrontations with demonic spirits affecting people and saw almost all of the individuals become free.

THE MYSTERY OF THE AGES

Paul declared that the church was a mystery hidden in God. The Holy Spirit, through the apostles and prophets of the early church, revealed this mystery. God's sacred secret was that the church would be made up of all ethnic groups as one new race in Him. Paul confessed that God was at work in him to preach the gospel to the nations. He also wanted to introduce them into the fellowship of the church:

> To me, who am less than the least of all the saints, this grace was given, that I should preach among the Gentiles the unsearchable riches of Christ, and to make all see what is the fellowship of the mystery, which from the beginning of the ages has been hidden in God who created all things through Jesus Christ. (Eph. 3:8–9 NKJV)

Paul revealed another of the mysterious purposes of the church: "To the intent that now the manifold wisdom of God might be made known by the church to the principalities and powers in the heavenly places" (Eph. 3:10 NKJV). One of God's purposes for the church is to impact "the principalities and powers" with the wisdom of God. God is determined to expose the demonic element hovering in heavenly places and defeat it through the church.

You see, the church must serve notice to the forces of hell. The body of Christ must declare the wisdom of God in saving and assembling the church. We are to take the manifold wisdom of God and rout the forces of darkness.

THE GATES OF HELL

In Jesus' first statement about the church, He declared, "Upon this rock I will build my church; and the gates of hell shall not prevail against it" (Matt. 16:18 KJV). In this verse, Jesus indicated that the church should fortify itself against the very gates of hell in order to rescue the captives. We are at war, yet Jesus has already won the victory at the cross of Calvary. Colossians 2:15 (NKJV) describes His triumph as He "disarmed principalities and powers."

Since we are fighting for a victory, let us look together at our battle strategy.

KNOW YOUR ENEMY

Paul named our enemy,

Finally, my brethren, be strong in the Lord and in the power of His might. Put on the whole armor of God, that you may be able to stand against the wiles of the devil. For we do not wrestle against flesh and blood, but against principalities, against powers, against the rulers of the darkness of this age, against spiritual hosts of wickedness in the heavenly places . . . Above all, taking the shield of faith with which you will be able to quench all the fiery darts of the wicked one. (Eph. 6:10–12, 16 NKJV)

The adversary is identified as the devil. The Greek word *diabolo* means to "cast through." He is the Satan of the Old Testament. He is the archangel who fell from glory and became the archfiend of hell. This is the one who is our enemy.

Many are oblivious to who the enemy is. They believe that the enemy is other individuals or personal problems. Someone has said, "We have met the enemy and he is us!" Often we are shooting at the wrong target.

I once read about a deer hunter whose wife finally persuaded him to take her along on a hunt. He positioned her on a stand and told her to watch for deer. He was halfway to his stand when he heard a gun shot. He went back and saw his wife holding the gun. A man standing nearby said nervously, "Yes, ma'am, he is your deer. Just let me get my saddle off!" She had shot at the wrong target. As Christians, we should not fight the wrong enemy.

BELIEVER: STAND READY!

As a child of God, you are instructed to notice Satan's wiles. The word *wiles* translates from the word *schemata* from which our English word *scheme* comes. It speaks of "plans made carefully." Satan has carefully laid plans and schemes to thwart the work of God.

He is a deceiver and a liar. Jesus called him the father of lies. He is the great perverter. According to the Bible, he looks like an angel of light.

You must also recognize his workers. We are warned, "For we do not wrestle against flesh and blood, but against principalities, against powers, against the rulers of the darkness of this age, against spiritual hosts of wickedness in the heavenly places" (Eph. 6:12 NKJV). These names are the various ranks of demonic forces, listed in a military order, with a battle plan to thwart the work of God. These forces can possess, obsess, and depress persons. They must be resisted.

In addition, you must avoid the weapons of Satan, your enemy. These weapons are specified as fiery darts or flaming missiles. The darts are designed to attack the inner person. They come against the mind, emotions, and will. He hurls guilt, doubt, worry, fear, hatred, and unbelief to try to undermine any work of God's Spirit in the life of the believer.

WHERE THE BATTLE RAGES

The battle takes place in three realms. *The first is in the place of worship,* which is in "the heavenlies." This is the place of Christ's exaltation where the believer sits with Him. We battle these invisible forces in relationship to our spiritual commitment and worship. In fact, the place of worship exists as the place of battle as well. The church should be a place of praise *and* a place of deliverance. Having one without the other can cause hurting and searching people to walk away from the church feeling empty and unsatisfied.

Cults and the occult capture many people for that reason. Satan gives them a counterfeit experience within the cult family. The false feeling of security and love that they experience tends to dull the empty ache inside. The religious realm is a place where Satan actively operates.

The battle rages in this present world, on our planet (Eph. 6:13). Our earth has been plunged into disaster, and disasters are often due to satanic control. In what other way can one explain the rise of Hitler and the inhumanity that took place during World War II, except to point to the evil one and his vicious agenda?

Our world is littered with the casualties of Satan. We are in an awful struggle for the minds and hearts of men. Today, Satan utilizes the media as a key part of his deceptive purposes. Music and entertainment have become valuable vehicles for him to proclaim his messages.

The battle also rages at the point of weakness. Satan attacks you at your most vulnerable point. He comes at you from your blind side. When Jesus had been hungry for forty days, Satan tempted Him to turn stones into bread.

Consider a husband and a wife who have been involved in a quarrel that has lasted over a period of days. Satan would see that as a key time to tempt one or both partners with an illicit affair. He works on our weaknesses to make us his slaves. He specializes in using alcohol, drugs, sex, tempers, and even personal likes and dislikes. He desires to destroy you.

ARMED AND READY

The believer needs weapons to stand against Satan. Let us read again Paul's description of the armor:

> Therefore take up the whole armor of God, that you may be able to withstand in the evil day, and having done all, to stand. Stand therefore, having girded your waist with truth, having put on the breastplate of righteousness, and having shod your feet with the preparation of the gospel of peace; above all, taking the shield of faith with which you will be able to quench all the fiery darts of the wicked one. And take the helmet of salvation, and the sword of the Spirit, which is the word of God. (Eph. 6:13–17 NKJV)

We are to put on the armor *finally*. The word for putting on the armor is an imperative, a once-and-for-all command. The Lord as our commander in chief has provided armor for us.

We are to put on the armor *fully*. God says to put on the "whole" armor. We are to put it all on. Paul was using the complete armor of the Roman foot soldier as a model, with each piece symbolizing some aspect of spiritual truth.

The belt of truth speaks of *personal integrity*, and the breastplate of righteousness speaks of *purity*, the righteousness of Jesus Christ.

The shoes speak of *stability* (v. 15). These shoes had hobnails in them to provide stability. The nails could be compared to the cleats found on the bottom of some athletic shoes—they provide better traction and enable the runner to maintain his balance when in action. The peace of the gospel helps us to keep our balance in the activity of life.

The shield of faith speaks of *humility* (v. 16). The soldier would kneel behind the large shield for protection. We kneel behind our shield of faith.

The helmet of salvation speaks of *victory* (v. 17). This speaks of the protection of the mind. When we get saved, we are protected from a deathblow. We must have this assurance in order to continue faithfully.

The sword of the Spirit speaks of the *Word of God.* This is our only offensive weapon. Our Lord used the weapon of the Word. Jesus fought Satan with Scripture and won. James 4:7 (NKJV) admonishes us, "Resist the devil and he will flee from you." George Duffield Jr. penned this wonderful hymn of warfare:

> Put on the gospel armor
> Each piece put on with care
> Where duty calls or danger
> Be ever watchful there. [1]

I read of an admiral in the Revolutionary War who, in the heat and confusion of battle, mistakenly used all of his ammunition shooting at a statue on the wall of the city he was besieging. When the time came for the real battle, he was helpless. Let us focus all of *our* weapons on Satan, the true enemy of our souls.

We must not forget that the call to battle in Ephesians 6:10 and following is preceded by Ephesians 5:18 (NKJV), which charges us to "be filled with the Spirit." Being filled with God's Spirit will bring you into conflict with the enemy. However, you can have confidence to know that the victory is yours. If you will stand in full armor, God will put the enemy to flight.

Right now, why don't you take these beginning steps to victory?

1. Confess every sin that has given the enemy a place in your life. "Neither give place to the devil," says the Scripture (Eph. 4:27 KJV). Satan can have a foothold only when you let him.

2. Ask God for a fresh filling of the Holy Spirit.

3. Speak out loud and claim every piece of the armor.

4. Find Scripture to strengthen you in the area of your attack. Swing the sword of God's Word by speaking it out loud against the enemy. The enemy cannot read your mind.

5. Command every force of darkness to leave your life.

6. Use the armor by confessing who you are in Jesus.

Now just speak your heart to your Father:

Lord, I am girded with the truth about myself. I am Your child accepted as beloved in Your sight. I am pure, Lord, because You have given me Your righteousness as my breastplate. Lord, I take a stand in the shoes You have given me, and I will not be moved. Lord, I lift up the mighty shield of faith against all the attacks of the enemy. I confess I am saved, and I wear the helmet of my security in Christ. I take Your Word, Lord, as a sword against every demonic force. I claim the victory that is mine. In Jesus' name. Amen.

Chapter 14

HE MAKES ME
LIE DOWN

$\mathcal{I}$s "falling out," being "slain in the spirit," or "resting in the Lord" a biblical practice? Is it a historical experience? What purpose does it serve? When does God cause people to "lie down"?

Perhaps you have asked these questions as you witnessed or heard about experiences of this nature. It is perfectly natural for Christians to inquire into the biblical nature of trances. It looks weird and seems strange, but beware of making the mistake of prematurely condemning this practice. We are told to search the Scriptures daily to see if what Paul was saying was true (Acts 17:11).

Before we search the Scriptures, read carefully the testimony of my wife, Paulette, as she tells of her unexpected falling out in front of five hundred women. She didn't desire this or ask God for this visitation.

The time was March 1997, when the Lee University Choir performed for a national taping at our church. A guest soloist, Judy Jacobs, sang a new song "Statement of Faith." The words rang so powerfully:

The words of her song rang so powerfully over the awestruck audience, from the young preschoolers to the senior saints. In an age when Christians are too often silent about their faith, Judy sang her beliefs with boldness, clarity, confidence, and authority that arrested us all to attention. This song was her personal testimony, and we knew it. She proclaimed her faith in God, the crucifixion, the resurrection, and Christ's return. She reminded us of our commitment to marriage, the family, the church, the Bible, and the God whose name we bear.

I felt God prompting me to invite her to speak at an upcoming Ladies' Night Out, a special meeting planned for the women of our church. As the director of women's ministries at our church for fourteen years, I have enjoyed watching the ways in which God ministers to and through women today.

During the next six months, the Women's Council and committee teams began preparing and praying for that special night. Our leaders prayed for a new level of anointing, ministry, and service of women, as well as a greater joy, a greater power, and a greater influence for God. We prayed for a "new thing." We prayed boldly and daily.

God gave me a special prayer promise in Matthew 11:12 (NKJV): "Now the kingdom of heaven suffers violence, and the violent take it by force." This prayer promise was a call for holy violence: to become militant for God by taking back our children, our homes, our futures, and claiming our deliverance. More than fifty leaders prayed this verse and claimed it for hurting and suffering women. We claimed it, we believed it, and we acted upon it. I even shared this verse with our entire congregation one Sunday morning. Excitement grew as the night approached.

Although our banquet hall seats only five hundred, that night the hall was full, and there was a waiting list of more than one hundred for tickets. Judy Jacobs sang and preached with power that was supernatural. We looked at each other in amazement as she called out her Scripture text for the night as Matthew 11:12. Out of all the verses in the whole Bible, she chose as her text our prayer promise! That alone brought the house down. An air of expectation filled the house, and we sat expecting God to move.

God's presence was real, and His deliverance was powerful. Our prayers had been answered. Half of the women in attendance gathered on the stage and around the podium to be prayed over that evening. Hurting hearts were mended, and the promises of God were claimed on behalf of erring children, torn marriages, and desperate situations.

As the mistress of ceremonies, I was preparing to close the worship service when suddenly Judy took the microphone back from me. Without touching me in any way, she began to prophesy over me, and I fell to the floor in front of five hundred women! No one was there to catch me; God simply let me down gently.

Now understand, this had never happened to me before! I was Baptist born, Baptist reared, Baptist educated, and Baptist wed. I had been a Baptist preacher's wife for thirty-one years, and I considered myself a very unlikely candidate for that type of experience. I am a high school English teacher, a classical musician, and a reserved southern lady who would never make a spectacle of myself in front of anyone. To my knowledge I have never embarrassed my God, my husband, or myself publicly. However, on this special night, I was slain in the Spirit and felt immobile under the heaviness of God. When finally I was able to rise, Ms. Jacobs handed me the microphone, and still in awe, I closed the service.

Why did God do that to me publicly? I don't know. I can only guess. What did it accomplish in my life?

First, I can tell you that freedom broke over me that night. The ropes and chains of tradition fell off me. God had done the unexpected in order to break the bondage of tradition and good works. For years I had been operating from guilt, legalistic rules, and religious rituals.

God caused me to lie down in green pastures. He restored my soul (Ps. 23). I possessed great peace and great joy. As I lay on the floor, I did not hear the prophecy over me; however, when I came up from that restful trance, I knew undeniably that the Lord had done a great thing for me, and I was glad, glad, so glad!

I knew that "I was not ashamed of the gospel of Christ for it is the power of God." God may have felt He needed to break my pride publicly and humble me before the women I served. He had chosen to speak over me a new ministry. Perhaps it was too much for me to receive, and so God insulated me with rest.

I also feel God may have chosen to use me to show His power to women who knew and trusted me, women who knew I would never imitate, seek after, or try to fake something supernatural.

Many of these women had known me for nineteen years and had followed my leadership. When I was praying that God would do a new thing for women on that night, I had no idea He would choose to do a public work through me.

I gained so much from that humbling, yet glorious experience. I gained continued revival, a greater thirst for God, a greater confidence in God's power, and a greater release for ministry. A militant faith rose inside me. Today, I really believe that "I can do all things through Christ who strengthens me" (Phil. 4:13 NKJV). Am I better for this? The answer is a resounding yes![1]

The focal point for Baptists when hearing a testimony like Paulette's is to respond, "Is that kind of thing biblical?" That is an appropriate question, for we must be grounded in Scripture for everything we believe, say, or do. Christians must be anchored firmly to the authority of Scripture. God does extraordinary, supernatural events, but He will never violate or depart from His holy Word.

You may call it "falling out," "resting in the Lord," or a "trance experience," but an honest study of the holy Scriptures absolutely validates these experiences as a part of God's supernatural visitation to man.

I am again recording the events as they occurred in Scripture. The Bible doesn't clearly commend the practice of falling out as a ritual of church worship. However, throughout this study, we must remember that God has ultimate control over our bodies—He created us. When He overwhelms us with His presence, unusual things may happen, and we must be careful not to reject something just because it is unusual.

In describing their experiences, people will often say that they are still conscious, yet totally engaged with the Lord. Many times a significant change occurs in the person's life as a result of the event. Let's look at the biblical precedent for this phenomenon.

OLD TESTAMENT REST

In Genesis 2:21, God caused a "deep sleep" to fall on Adam so He could remove a rib in order to fashion woman. He then closed Adam's side. He performed all of this surgery while Adam slept. He not only removed the rib, but also healed Adam's body after the surgery. Many have wondered if perhaps Adam had a scar on his side as a reminder that Eve was a gift to him. (We know that the Second Adam had His side ripped open and still bears the scar showing His love to us.) Adam felt God's touch on his life in his physical body.

What God did then, He can do now. During a "falling out" time, God can perform surgery and healing for people in a spiritual, emotional, mental, or physical way.

In Genesis 15:12, God put Abram into a deep sleep. God then prophesied or spoke the future over Abram's resting spirit. He told Abram that his descendants would be slaves in Egypt for four hundred years. After that period of bondage, He said Abram's descendants would be delivered and would march out of Egypt with great wealth. Not only did God prophesy the future, but He also promised that Abram would live to a great old age and would be buried with his fathers. Abram listened in his trance and heard the voice of God.

In Numbers 24, God used a mercenary false prophet, a mere magician and sorcerer, to speak the word of God. Balaam had made a deal with Balak, the king of Moab. For big bucks, Balaam agreed to curse the children of Israel publicly. Verses 4 and 16 (NKJV) state of Balaam: "[He] sees the vision of the Almighty . . . [he] falls down, with eyes wide open."

Each time Balaam tried to curse the people of God, he fell down with his eyes wide open, seeing a vision from almighty God. Instead of curses, *blessings* for the nation of Israel came rushing out of his mouth! That happened not once, but *three* times. Angrily, King Balak shouted that the deal was off. Balaam would get no money from him! The fourth time Balaam opened his mouth, he prophesied: "A Star shall come out of Jacob; a Scepter shall rise out of Israel" (v. 17 NKJV).

In a trance, the unbelieving follower of witchcraft saw a vision of God and prophesied the word of God. How amazing to consider that through a trance, God used Balaam's mouth for His glory!

Even today, God can and does turn unbelieving occult followers into preachers of His gospel. Several months ago, a teenager stood in our service and gave testimony to Christ's intervention in her life. She and her friends had become deeply involved in wicca, or supposed "white" magic. She had soon become dissatisfied with it and began to experiment with more blatant occult practices. She found herself gripped by something she could no longer control, and drug and alcohol abuse added to her problems.

The tormented young lady was put in contact with our deliverance counseling ministry. She was gloriously saved and set free, and now gives her testimony to warn others of the dangers of playing around with the lure of power that Satan uses to entangle souls.

The prophet Ezekiel had several experiences in which God visited him in a trance. In Ezekiel 1:28 (NKJV), he described the first of them and recorded his response: "This was the appearance of the likeness of the glory of the LORD. So when I saw it, I fell on my face."

Ezekiel 2:2 reveals that the prophet saw a vision and heard a voice when he fell on his face. The voice commissioned him to a ministry to a rebellious people, and the voice told Ezekiel not to be afraid. While Ezekiel was in a trance, God called him to a new work—a new ministry.

He described another supernatural experience: "The glory of the LORD stood there, like the glory which I saw by the River Chebar; and I fell on my face" (Ezek. 3:23 NKJV).

In Ezekiel 3, he saw a vision of God as fire and brightness. In the same passage and as part of that same visitation, God told the prophet to be mute, unable to speak rebuke to the rebellious nation. At an appointed time when God spoke, then Ezekiel would also be free to speak: "He stretched out the form of a hand, and took me by a lock of my hair; and the Spirit lifted me up between earth and heaven, and brought me in visions of God to Jerusalem" (Ezek. 8:3 NKJV). There He showed Ezekiel many abominations that his people were committing against their God.

These texts alone convince us that spiritual, physical, and emotional manifestations of the Holy Spirit took place in the life of the prophet. Yet one of the most intriguing stories in all of Scripture further verifies the supernatural work of God in Ezekiel's ministry. Ezekiel 37:1 (NKJV) tells how Ezekiel was introduced to the valley of dry bones: "The hand of the LORD came upon me and brought me out in the Spirit of the LORD, and set me down in the midst of the valley; and it was full of bones." God took Ezekiel in the Spirit to another place. God revealed spiritual truth to him concerning the captivity of the Jewish people.

Ezekiel wasn't the only prophet to have the Spirit of God overpower him. Daniel said,

> So [Gabriel] came near where I stood, and when he came I was afraid and fell on my face; but he said to me, "Understand, son of man, that the vision refers to the time of the end." Now, as he was speaking with me, I was in a deep sleep with my face to the ground; but he touched me, and stood me upright. (Dan. 8:17–18 NKJV)

During the trance experience, Daniel heard the voice of an angel speaking about the end of time. Verse 27 states that when the trance was over, Daniel fainted and was sick several days.

FALLING OUT IN THE NEW TESTAMENT

The New Testament also records many biblical accounts that support this strange and unusual phenomenon labeled "falling out."

The first reference is Matthew 17:1–6, which is an account of the Transfiguration. On the mountain, God showed three disciples what the significance of the Law and Prophets was and that Jesus was greater and the fulfillment of both. When the disciples heard that, they fell to the ground with faces down. They were terrified and totally overwhelmed by both the words of the revelation and the way it was delivered. Jesus touched them and reassured them gently.

In another account in Matthew, the soldiers who were guarding Jesus' tomb were literally paralyzed with fear when the angel appeared sitting on the stone that was rolled away. The guards were so afraid of the angel that they "shook for fear of him, and became like dead men" (28:4 NKJV). Their fear (reverence) in the presence of angels made them fall as though they were slain. Notice that in the presence of God's power, both believers and unbelievers seem to be unable to stand.

The book of John tells the account of unbelievers falling in the presence of something holy. In the account Judas and the Roman soldiers had come to arrest Jesus. Jesus identified Himself, saying, "I am He" or "I AM." The power in His words caused the soldiers to move away from Jesus, and then they suddenly fell to the ground (John 18:1–6).

In the book of Acts, the apostle Paul recorded two separate visitations from God. The first encounter took place as he was on the road to Damascus with papers to arrest more Christians. Paul (or Saul, as he was known before his salvation) was responsible for the deaths of many believers. In Acts 9:4, a blinding light from heaven appeared and seized Saul. He heard a voice from heaven and fell to the ground blinded. His fellow travelers also heard the voice, but saw nothing except Saul's response and blindness: "Then he fell to the ground, and heard a voice saying to him, 'Saul, Saul, why are you persecuting Me?' And he said, 'Who are You, Lord?' Then the Lord said, 'I am Jesus, whom you are persecuting'" (Acts 9:4–5 NKJV). Here again we see clear evidence of falling out as a natural response to a divine revelation.

Paul arose from that experience blinded for several days. Although his physical sight was temporarily gone, his spiritual eyes could see clearly. In a trance, he received confrontation and correction from Jesus. Paul recounted this experience before the Jews in Jerusalem (Acts 22) and again before King Agrippa (Acts 26).

Another encounter experienced by Paul is recorded in Acts 22:17–18 (NKJV): "Now it happened, when I [Paul] returned to Jerusalem and was praying in the temple, that I was in a trance and saw Him [Jesus] saying to me, 'Make haste and get out of Jerusalem quickly, for they will not receive your testimony concerning Me.'"

Paul definitely heard the voice of Jesus. Paul was in a trance. We do not know whether or not he had fallen to the ground, but he was out of consciousness and totally absorbed or engaged in communing with Christ. The purpose of the trance was to give Paul deliverance from his enemies. The experience happened to him in church. God needed to give Paul specific instructions, for more than forty Jewish leaders had sworn an oath that they would neither eat nor drink until they had killed Paul. God supernaturally revealed that He had other plans for Paul!

Acts 10:10–17 (NKJV) records yet another apostle's experience. Peter had gone out onto a housetop to pray while his hosts were preparing dinner. There he "fell into a trance." In the vision, Peter saw a sheet let down from heaven with all kinds of animals on it. The voice in the vision said, "Rise, Peter; kill and eat." Peter responded by saying, "Not so, Lord! For I have never eaten anything common or unclean." The voice rebuked Peter, saying that what God had cleansed, he should never call common. The exchange happened three times. God used the vision to call Peter to minister to a man named Cornelius in Caesarea. God was making Peter ready for a new ministry to the Gentiles. Peter heeded the vision that called him to a new task.

The whole book of Revelation is a vision of God's glory to the beloved apostle John. Revelation 1:1 (NKJV) gives this introduction to the book: "The Revelation of Jesus Christ, which God gave Him to show His servants—things which must shortly take place. And He sent and signified it by His angel to His servant John."

Revelation 1:10 (NKJV) tells of another experience of John: "I was in the Spirit on the Lord's Day, and I heard behind me a loud voice, as of a trumpet."

Revelation 1:17 (NKJV) tells us more: "And when I saw Him, I fell at His feet as dead. But He laid His right hand on me, saying to me, 'Do not be afraid; I am the First and the Last.'"

John in his vision saw many things and heard the voice of Jesus. He was a witness to the word of God and a witness to the testimony of Jesus. He saw, heard, and obeyed the heavenly vision.

NOTES FROM HISTORY

Here again are the great revivalists from history who observed instances of resting in the Lord.

Jonathan Edwards, the main instrument and theologian of the Great Awakening in America (1725–60), said in his "Account of the Revival of Religion in North Hampton in 1740–42":

> Many have had their religious affections raised far beyond what they have ever had before; and there were some instances of persons lying in a sort of trance, remaining perhaps for a whole twenty-four hours motionless, and with their senses locked up: but in the meantime under strong imaginations, as though they went to heaven and had there a vision of glorious and delightful objects.[2]

Charles Finney (1792–1875) was one of the most powerful revivalists since the Reformation. At a country place named Sodom, in the state of New York, Finney gave one address in which he described the condition of Sodom before God destroyed it:

> I had not spoken in this strain more than a quarter of an hour when an awful solemnity seemed to settle upon them: the congregation began to fall from their seats in every direction, and cried for mercy. If I had a sword in each hand, I could not have cut them down as fast as they fell. Nearly the whole congregation was either on their knees or prostrate, I should think, in less than two minutes from the shock that fell upon them. Every one prayed who was able to speak at all.[3]

A SPIRITUAL TIME-OUT

I often think of the paraphrase of the notable theologian Saint Augustine's statement, "Love God and do what you want." This implies that if you really love God, you will want what He wants, and you will obey the law without the law. Using this same idea, we can say what is not contradictory to Scripture is allowed today. Jesus did more miracles and wonders than we know about. John closed his gospel with these words, "And there are also many other things that Jesus did, which if they were written one by one, I suppose that even the world itself could not contain the books that would be written. Amen" (John 21:25 NKJV).

I believe we are nearing the end times, experiencing a latter rain revival. In Israel, farmers can expect an early rain around planting season, and a late rain around the harvest season. These are often used in Scripture as symbols of spiritual awakening.

In these days of a latter rain revival, God is doing what He did in the book of Acts. We do not seek signs and wonders. We seek God's face. We seek to know Him in the power of His resurrection. This may require wide latitude in both charismatic and liturgical worship. When we seek Him, we will find Him, and He may choose to reveal Himself in signs and wonders.

What does God do when you fall out in a trance? God does exactly what He wants to do. His ways are not our ways, but we know that "He doeth all things well"! In every case, Jesus accomplishes a deeper work in the believer. He may perform surgery; heal your body; prophesy; give a promise; speak a strange word out of your mouth; send an angel; give instruction, correction, or deliverance; or call you to a new ministry. Whatever He does is communication from the Spirit of God to the spirit of man—Spirit-to-spirit contact. This bypasses your mind, will, emotions, thoughts, carnal desires, limitations, and demonic strongholds.

I like to think of falling out as a time-out with the Lord. If you are a parent, you may be familiar with that term. Little children are often placed in a time-out corner or chair in order to think about what they have done or failed to do. They are isolated from a group to calm their busy little bodies.

In the same way, we may need a time-out from our busyness. Our heavenly Coach may choose to take us out of the game temporarily. He may pull us aside to say a word of praise for a job well done. Our heavenly Coach may need to say, "Come away and rest a while!" He may have a new play or assignment for us, or He may change the game plan altogether. The Father may sense that we are hurt and need time for healing. Whatever the reason for a time-out with your heavenly Coach, listen to Him, trust Him, for it will always be for your good.

Part 5

A RELEASED CHURCH

Chapter 15

QUENCH NOT
THE SPIRIT

$\mathcal{P}$aul had several brief exhortations for the Thessalonian Christians, and we find one of those recorded in 1 Thessalonians 5:19. It is interesting to see how different English translations and paraphrases treat this verse:

> Do not quench the Spirit. (NKJV)
> Do not put out the Spirit's fire. (NIV)
> Do not smother the Holy Spirit. (TLB)

The word *quench* translates from a Greek word that means "to extinguish a flame" or "to suppress or stifle." Its tense in the original language could better be translated, "Do not ever put out the fire of the Holy Spirit." It requires continuous action and is a continuing command.

The following verse indicates that some held the prophetic word given by the Spirit in the church to be contemptible. They despised what happened that was out of their control: "Do not despise prophecies" (1 Thess. 5:20 NKJV).

You see, it is possible to throw cold water on someone else's passion for Christ. We are told that never under any circumstance are we to suppress the genuine work of the Holy Spirit.

A FIRE PUT OUT

Earlier in this book, I told of my first encounter with a demonized young man at a summer youth camp. A mighty outpouring of God marked the entire week, but the aftermath proved to be a spiritual battle.

After we returned from the camp, our association of churches began to hold monthly youth rallies. The Saturday night events often lasted several hours into the night, and lives were being profoundly touched. However, adults soon began to complain. They felt the kids were getting "too Christian." Their enthusiasm was spilling over into churches that were used to more quiet, orderly services. Before long, the legalists prevailed, and the meetings were taken over by "old guard" leadership. The fire quickly burned out.

A few months later, the same parents who complained about the late-night youth meetings were hosting all-night prom parties for their kids, some even including beer drinking. How sad it was to have watched the fires of passion for Jesus quenched by the tepid waters of tradition!

QUENCHING FIRE IN OTHERS

As the years passed, I became what I thought I never would, a professional, legalistic, Christian leader. I even quenched the spirit of my own daughter Heather. Earlier in the book I told about putting out the fire in Heather's life. Here is her story:

When my father asked me to tell my story, it was hard to decide where to begin and where to end. My story is still being written and I'm just not sure where it began. The natural place to begin is childhood and mine was a happy and healthy one. I was the second of three children in a Christian home with loving parents. I was overall a "good" child; I made good grades, obeyed my parents, and was in church at every possible opportunity. I was also involved in every possible church activity.

As I grew older church became less and less appealing to me. I became rebellious as a teenager and I hated going to church. I felt as the preacher's kid I was under constant criticism and scrutiny. I have never fit the mold of the "perfect Christian," which is what I felt was expected of me as the preacher's kid. Anything I did was magnified much more than the child of someone who was not in the limelight. The older and more rebellious I became, the more I felt that church would never be the place for me (even with my upbringing!). I knew I would never feel comfortable there. I wanted something that was real, and church to me seemed superficial and plastic. In my rebellion and search for something more, I grew farther and farther away from God.

Even though I was withdrawing myself from God, the church, and religion, God, of course, was not abandoning me. He sent an angel in the form of a youth worker; her name was Becky. She knew that I, like others in my youth group, needed more, much more than Southern Baptist religion. We needed to feel the power of God's love for us and His unconditional acceptance and forgiveness. We needed to know that we could live in freedom and peace.

She took several of us on a weekend retreat that was nondenominational and included teenagers from all different areas around our city. I had at this point been on many retreats with my church youth group and I didn't think this one would be any different from those.

I could not have been more wrong. The purpose of the retreat was to experience God's love and rejoice in it. That's all. Dozens of people volunteered to cook delicious food for us, keep up a twenty-four-hour-a-day prayer vigil for us, wake us in the mornings with singing and fresh flowers, and lead sessions of praise.

These people were for the most part complete strangers to all of us. I couldn't believe I actually enjoyed it. I felt loved and accepted because everyone involved was real. There were no phony or pious masks, just genuine kindness. This was the first time in my life that I realized what being a Christian really meant. It certainly had nothing to do with religion or rules. I feel that this is what God really had in mind, and what His Son, Jesus, tried to show the world not only in His death but also in His daily life. I realized that *Christian* is an adjective, as defined in Webster's: "showing a gentle, humble, helpful spirit."

This retreat and realization changed my heart instantly, but it took a few more years to change my life. Once I had realized what being a Christian really meant, it became a thousand times harder to actually follow through with it. I am still learning and growing as a Christian in my daily life, but I no longer strive to be someone else's definition of a perfect Christian. Galatians 5:22–23 (NKJV) says, "But the fruit of the Spirit is love, joy, peace, longsuffering, kindness, goodness, faithfulness, gentleness, self-control." God has given me the freedom to experience these so I strive to live by the Spirit and keep in step with the Spirit (Gal. 5:25) on a daily basis.[1]

Heather was too kind in her account to tell you, but my religious pride and prejudices would not embrace the new work that God had done in her. I couldn't understand why she had never responded to my ministry. My pride was hurt. I missed one of the great spiritual moments of her life because I was so empty.

HOW DOES ONE QUENCH THE SPIRIT?

First, you may quench the Spirit by ignoring the things of God. A fire left unattended will soon go out. You must personally give attention to the things of the Spirit if your passion is to stay alive. Almost anything alive will die from lack of attention. You must be proactive toward the Holy Spirit.

The Spirit may be quenched by someone else's influence in your life. You've probably come to realize that certain folks tend to be spiritual fire extinguishers. Critical people quench the Spirit of God. Their words, like sharp icicles, freeze out the fire of revival in a heart.

In addition, people with a spirit of performance may quench the Spirit. When there are manifestations of the Holy Spirit, some persons may try to imitate in the flesh or through emotion what the Spirit is doing. The service then loses its focus or becomes a parade of flesh. The Spirit of God is then quenched.

Satan, if given place, can certainly quench the Spirit. Satan may show up as a critic, but more often than not he will show up as a counterfeit. Second Corinthians 11:14 (NKJV) reminds us, "And no wonder! For Satan himself transforms himself into an angel of light."

Satan's demons may move someone to show false manifestation. In this way, confusion is sown, and the Holy Spirit quenched. At one time a man who attended our church would shout out loud at inappropriate times in a service, often disrupting a soloist or interrupting the preaching. He was called in for loving correction, but he reacted with extreme hostility and left the church. Several years later we discovered that he was master of an occult fraternity.

Very commonly, fear can quench the Spirit of God. In Paul's second letter to Timothy we see the cruel work of the spirit of fear: "Therefore I remind you to stir up the gift of God which is in you through the laying on of my hands. For God has not given us a spirit of fear, but of power and of love and of a sound mind" (1:6–7 NKJV).

He reminded the young pastor to "stir up the gift of God." This could be translated "fan the flame of the charisma, which is in you." Fear had tried to rob Timothy of power, love, and a sound mind. We should not allow the spirit of fear or timidity to put out the fire of God's charisma given to us all.

Of course, a departure from the Bible can quench the Spirit. True worship will strike a balance between the divine Word and the divine wind of the Spirit.

Both truth and Spirit are needed for God's power to be unleashed: "But the hour is coming, and now is, when the true worshipers will worship the Father in spirit and truth; for the Father is seeking such to worship Him. God is Spirit, and those who worship Him must worship in spirit and truth" (John 4:23–24 NKJV).

An unwillingness to change can quench the Spirit of God. Methods and tradition can become confused with Scripture. Listen to Jesus' warning in Matthew 15:9 (NKJV): "In vain they worship Me, teaching as doctrines the commandments of men." *The Living Bible* says it this way: "Their worship is worthless, for they teach their man-made laws instead of those from God."

When we get stuck in the past and long for the way it used to be before God's power fell, then we strip the Word of its miracle-working power. When we dull the blade of the two-edged sword with our traditions, the Word can no longer pierce as deeply into our hearts.

HOW TO REKINDLE THE FLAME

To restore lost power, you must fall in love with Jesus again. Rejoice again at His birth! Thrill again at His power! Weep at His crucifixion! Shout over His resurrection! Live expecting His return!

Furthermore, hang out with Spirit-filled people. Stay around people who encourage you. Negative people will pull you down.

You should strive for a Bible-based, praise-saturated, and prayer-empowered lifestyle. Make your home a place where God is worshiped. As you drive to work or school, fill your car with praise music and Bible teaching.

In addition, go to a church that is moving with the Spirit of God, even if it doesn't carry your label. Don't expect a church to change to suit you. If you have waited and prayed for several years and it still seems like an ice rink (people going in circles within a frozen atmosphere!), go to a place where you feel God is at work.

It is important to learn to live and give by faith. Faith brings the wonder back to the Christian life. Learn to hear God and trust Him for resources. Learn to be a channel of blessing to others.

Finally, find an outlet of ministry through which you can serve others. Discover your spiritual gifts and go for it in the name of Jesus. Reach out to the lost, the helpless, the hurting, and the homeless. Touch someone else with the fire of God in your life, and rather than quench the flame of the Spirit, you will watch it spread like wildfire.

Chapter 16

RIVERS OF
LIVING WATER

While I was recuperating from recent minor surgery, my oldest daughter, Kelli, brought me some videos to view. Among them was the movie *A River Runs Through It*.[1] The setting of the movie was the breathtakingly beautiful Montana wilderness. The theme of the movie was the life experience of a Presbyterian minister's family. The story carefully highlighted the dramatic differences in the personalities of family members.

As the plot returned again and again to a beautiful, wild, rushing river, we watched the minister's young boys learn to fly-fish and listened in as they were taught lessons about God and creation. Both boys struggled with life, one being an avid bookworm and the other a wild and free spirit. Both tragedy and joy followed the family. Yet flowing in the center of it all, and I believe, standing as a symbol of their faith, was the river. At that river, worries faded, differences disappeared, grudges were forgotten, and challenges were renewed.

I know of such a river as well. Jesus spoke of a river that should flow from all of our hearts.

WATER FROM THE ROCK

"If anyone thirsts, let him come to Me and drink. He who believes in Me, as the Scripture has said, out of his heart will flow rivers of living water." But this He spoke concerning the Spirit, whom those believing in Him would receive; for the Holy Spirit was not yet given, because Jesus was not yet glorified. (John 7:37–39 NKJV)

Jesus spoke those words during the Feast of Tabernacles. It was the feast during which the Jews were supposed to reflect on their time of wandering between Egypt and the promised land. They lived in tents or tabernacles to symbolize the years when their nation was homeless. They recalled such miracles as the parting of the Red Sea, the pillar of fire by day and cloud by night, the manna from heaven, and the water from the rock.

Jesus was standing in the crowd when the priests were returning from the Brook Kidron, preparing for one of these rituals. The particular exercise involved going to the brook and drawing out water in golden bowls. They would then pour the water out before the people while chanting:

And in that day you will say:
"O LORD, I will praise You;
Though You were angry with me,
Your anger is turned away, and You comfort me.
Behold, God is my salvation,
I will trust and not be afraid;
'For YAH, the LORD, is my strength and song;
He also has become my salvation.'"
Therefore with joy you will draw water
From the wells of salvation.

And in that day you will say:
"Praise the LORD, call upon His name;
Declare His deeds among the peoples,
Make mention that His name is exalted.
Sing to the LORD,
For He has done excellent things;
This is known in all the earth.
Cry out and shout, O inhabitant of Zion,
For great is the Holy One of Israel in your midst!" (Isa. 12:1–6 NKJV)

The priests had just spoken those required words, "With joy shall we draw water out of the well of salvation." Precisely at that high moment of religious ritual, Jesus cried out with a loud voice, "If anyone thirsts, let him come to Me and drink" (John 7:37 NKJV).

You see, across the years, Israel had moved from reality to ritual. They could no longer believe God for the direction and comfort of the shekinah glory cloud. They knew their ancestors had been given heat in the nights and coolness in the day under the shadow of the cloud of God's presence. But now, they could only pretend He was there. They no longer expected miracles of manna and meat. Religion was rules and rituals without a relationship with the supernatural God.

Just take a moment and grasp the beauty of this moment: standing in their midst and inviting them to His supernatural life was the very One who had guided, guarded, fed, and given their forefathers the water in the wilderness. Remember, the ritual in which they had been involved just before Jesus spoke was a ritual to commemorate that Old Testament miracle.

In 1 Corinthians 10:4 (NKJV), Paul identified that Old Testament water-giving rock as Christ: "And all drank the same spiritual drink.

For they drank of that spiritual Rock that followed them, and that Rock was Christ." It is fascinating to note that Paul said the Rock followed them. In other words, wherever they camped, the Rock giving forth water showed up.

LIVING WITHOUT POWER

What do *you* do when you can no longer sense the leadership of the Holy Spirit? What happens to Christianity when faith in a miracle-working God is embarrassing? How do you "do church" when you can't get water from a rock anymore?

Religion tries to substitute rituals and rules for the real thing. It attempts to relegate miracles and manifestations of the Spirit to the past, due to an embarrassing lack of power in the present. It is easier to talk about how wonderful it used to be or how wonderful heaven is going to be than to deal with the awful absence of the power of God in the here and now.

In the same way that the priests carried their golden bowls back and forth from the river in empty ritual, so are many today trying to fill their thirsty souls with religious talk and traditions, knowing that His presence is gone.

People in powerless churches tend to let the sick know that they are thinking about them instead of crying out to God for their healing. Individuals with strongholds such as depression, fear, lust, anger, and bitterness are left to secular solutions, often paying hundreds (even thousands) of dollars for counseling and drug prescriptions. Their powerless churches operate in the energy of the flesh with no word or direction from God. People's souls are left dry and thirsty.

The good news is that Jesus still cries out today, inviting the thirsty to come to Him.

THE RIVER OF THE SPIRIT

John told us that Jesus' "river of living water" is the Holy Spirit flowing out of a person. Jesus is the One who gives us a drink of His Spirit. That drink taps us into a veritable river of divine power. God's Spirit comes *within* us, but is also released *out* of us.

The apostle John recorded Jesus' words regarding how this river released in our lives was prophesied in the Old Testament: "He who believes in Me, as the Scripture has said, out of his heart will flow rivers of living water" (John 7:38 NKJV). I believe that here Jesus was speaking about the vivid scene described in Ezekiel 47:

> Then he brought me back to the door of the temple; and there was water, flowing from under the threshold of the temple toward the east, for the front of the temple faced east; the water was flowing from under the right side of the temple, south of the altar. He brought me out by way of the north gate, and led me around on the outside to the outer gateway that faces east; and there was water, running out on the right side. And when the man went out to the east with the line in his hand, he measured one thousand cubits, and he brought me through the waters; the water came up to my ankles. Again he measured one thousand and brought me through the waters; the water came up to my knees. Again he measured one thousand and brought me through; the water came up to my waist. Again he measured one thousand, and it was a river that I could not cross; for the water was too deep, water in which one must swim, a river that could not be crossed. He said to me, "Son of man, have you seen this?" Then he brought me and returned me to the bank of the river. When I returned, there, along the bank of the river, were very many trees on one side and the other. Then he said to me: "This water flows toward the eastern region, goes down into the

valley, and enters the sea. When it reaches the sea, its waters are healed. And it shall be that every living thing that moves, wherever the rivers go, will live. There will be a very great multitude of fish, because these waters go there; for they will be healed, and everything will live wherever the river goes." (Ezek. 47:1–9 NKJV)

Here a river is seen gushing out of the temple. In the Old Testament, God had a temple for His people. In the New Testament, God has a people for His temple! Remember the words found in 1 Corinthians 6:19 (NKJV): "Or do you not know that your body is the temple of the Holy Spirit who is in you, whom you have from God, and you are not your own?" Out of individuals and out of the gathered church there should be flowing a river like we see in Ezekiel's vision. Just as the river in his vision grew larger and deeper as it made its way toward the sea, so will a real move of God grow larger and deeper over time.

As Ezekiel tagged along on the "measuring expedition," he began ankle-deep and gradually moved into the river until he was in over his head. You may know from your own experience with water that as long as your feet are planted on the ground, you stay in control. However, once you get in over your head, the river totally takes over. In the same way, the river that flows out of a believer will control and carry him on in the will of God. Giving up control to Jesus is a part of surrendering to His fullness.

RIVERS OF LIVING WATER

As the river flowed onward in Ezekiel's vision, it brought life for death and fruitfulness for barrenness; even the salty Dead Sea came alive with fish. The work of the Holy Spirit released from a Spirit-filled church can flow over wider and deeper into the dark, dirty, dry, and dead places of society. Into those places life can come by the power of God.

A river of life is flowing out of every yielded Christian. When individuals in a church get together, the river becomes larger. When churches break down the walls of sectarianism, the river becomes a flood of awakening and revivals.

Some rivers are flowing that are sweet with the fragrance of praise and worship. Out of other believers there are flowing rivers that are rich with spiritual gifts and graces. Others release rivers of anointed preaching and teaching. Then there are those who allow their rivers to flow into the inner cities to touch poor and helpless people. Still others allow the river to flow into other needy nations.

I believe the latter rain is falling. Many churches are reaching floodtide. The river is washing over denominational borders and will soon explode into awakening. My appeal to all is to allow the Holy Spirit to do His work in His way. Determine with David to be a friend to all who are friends of Jesus Christ: "I am a companion of all who fear You, and of those who keep Your precepts" (Ps. 119:63 NKJV).

Chapter 17

THE CHURCH
OF THE FUTURE

Our Lord's ministry was characterized by compassion. He came to "save that which was lost" (Matt. 18:11 NKJV). He was a Shepherd looking with compassion on a torn and scattered flock. He had compassion on those whose mental health had been stolen by the forces of darkness. Jesus cared about the sick and infirm. Jesus warned the religious crowd about mistreating elderly people. Jesus cared for children and blessed them. He didn't condemn sinners; He forgave them. He touched and healed the outcasts of society, such as people with leprosy.

Today's church prefers to look good on the outside. You can walk into most suburban churches and be entertained by good music, hear a solid Bible exposition, and think everyone has got it together. We want our churches to look good and reach the "right" kind of people.

If you could pull back the curtain over the hearts of many of those who attend your church, you would undoubtedly see unprecedented pain and spiritual bondage. What kind of salvation are we offering to our people? Primarily, we are offering them a ticket out of hell and a promise that heaven will make up for all of our problems here. But that is only part of the truth!

Jesus said, "I have come that they may have life, and that they may have it more abundantly" (John 10:10 NKJV). From this verse, we learn that the Bible promises more than we are delivering in the average church. Many evangelicals are asking why fewer than 50 percent of people on their rolls attend services anymore. Also, they ask why the charismatic church is packed and theirs is emptying. Our answers may vary from accusing the charismatics of sensationalism to bemoaning our geographical location. The truth is that too many of us have failed to deliver what the Bible promises to every believer.

SALVATION IS A DELIVERANCE

New Testament salvation is no less than spiritual emancipation. Paul's teaching made this very clear: "He has delivered us from the power of darkness and conveyed us into the kingdom of the Son of His love, in whom we have redemption through His blood, the forgiveness of sins" (Col. 1:13–14 NKJV).

All who are truly saved have been delivered from the authority of the enemy. Yet many have never discovered their wonderful position in Christ. Paul addressed this issue in Ephesians 1:17–2:7 (NKJV):

That the God of our Lord Jesus Christ, the Father of glory, may give to you the spirit of wisdom and revelation in the knowledge of Him, the eyes of your understanding being enlightened; that you may know what is the hope of His calling, what are the riches of the glory of His inheritance in the saints, and what is the exceeding greatness of His power toward us who believe, according to the working of His mighty power which He worked in Christ when He

raised Him from the dead and seated Him at His right hand in the
heavenly places, far above all principality and power and might and
dominion, and every name that is named, not only in this age but
also in that which is to come. And He put all things under His feet,
and gave Him to be head over all things to the church, which is His
body, the fullness of Him who fills all in all. And you He made
alive, who were dead in trespasses and sins, in which you once
walked according to the course of this world, according to the
prince of the power of the air, the spirit who now works in the sons
of disobedience, among whom also we all once conducted ourselves
in the lusts of our flesh, fulfilling the desires of the flesh and of the
mind, and were by nature children of wrath, just as the others. But
God, who is rich in mercy, because of His great love with which He
loved us, even when we were dead in trespasses, made us alive
together with Christ (by grace you have been saved), and raised us
up together, and made us sit together in the heavenly places in
Christ Jesus, that in the ages to come He might show the exceeding riches of His grace in His kindness toward us in Christ Jesus.

Many believers have been wounded by others or injured by their
own past sin. They live under bondages of fear, bitterness, lust,
depression, poverty, rebellion, and a host of other strongholds, some
of which were passed down through their families. So often as we
attempt to disciple people who are carrying multiple chains on their
lives, we may find that our efforts are an added burden to them. Jesus
Christ demonstrated the proper order in His ministry to oppressed
people: first drive out the demons and then start renewal.

In the church we must encourage people in their faith. Our
church has an encourager ministry where a believer is taken through
"The Seven Steps to Freedom." This wonderful material is a part of
Dr. Neil Anderson's book *The Bondage Breaker.*[1]

This ministry was birthed when I invited Dr. Anderson to come to our church for a seminar. For eight days nearly one thousand adults found true freedom in Jesus Christ from the enemy's strongholds. Each year, hundreds of people are set free from their past through our biblical encouragement ministry.

THE HOPE OF THIS GENERATION

The young people and young adults of today are experience oriented. They plunge headfirst into everything. Woe to the leader who thinks he can do ministry with just the facts. Members of this generation believe in the supernatural. They are also ungrounded in biblical truth. Therefore, they are ripe for being captured by a cult. The church must become a heart place as well as a head place. These young people expect to be touched and prayed for. They want to participate in worship. They do not want to be an audience. They are more into relationships than rules.

That was what the ministry of Jesus was all about. Jesus was most interested in connecting with people's hearts. Jesus loved to celebrate. Jesus liked having children around. Jesus liked to touch and be touched.

THE CHURCH OF THE FUTURE

The church of the future must meet this generation where it is. What will be the characteristics of this growing church?

A PLACE WHERE JESUS IS WELCOME

The church will not simply talk about Jesus, but will welcome Jesus to do His ministry in power. The Lord Jesus had to return to heaven, but promised to return again to us through the person of the

Holy Spirit. Nothing can take the place of the Holy Spirit's presence in the life of the church. Like Samson, today's churches "shake" themselves as before, yet they do not know that the Lord has departed (Judg. 16:20).

As recorded in the Gospels, Jesus walked on the water. He appeared in such a different form that not even His disciples recognized Him. They cried out, "It is a ghost." Often when Jesus manifests Himself in ways the church has not seen before, fear may rise. Yet Peter dared to step out and risk all for this "water-walking Jesus."

Suppose that the disciples grabbed their Bibles consisting of the thirty-nine books of the Old Testament. They found no record that the Messiah would walk on the water. Then, thumping their Bibles, they rejected Him. It would be probable that their failure to act in faith would cause them to be caught and die in the storm.

Jesus will not contradict Scripture, but neither is He confined to Scripture. Where there is no clear verse to tell you how to act, there will always be a principle. Jesus is not confined to the Bible; He releases the Bible's truth for us.

Jesus' ministry is poignantly described in Acts 10:38 (NKJV): "How God anointed Jesus of Nazareth with the Holy Spirit and with power, who went about doing good and healing all who were oppressed by the devil, for God was with Him."

A PLACE WHERE THE GREAT COMMISSION IS TAKEN SERIOUSLY

This church will not confine its witness to its own kind. The church that is to survive must die to itself and its culture. Every wall must come down between the classes, the races, the genders, and the denominations. Kingdom work will be the priority. The church will reach from the inner city to the ends of the earth.

A PLACE WHERE WORSHIP IS REAL AND POWERFUL

People will not be spectators at a performance, but participants who celebrate the presence of Jesus. They may sing, clap, move in rhythm, shout, laugh, or weep before the Lord. They may quietly meditate and participate thoughtfully in the elements of a service, not in mere repetition, but in deep awareness of the presence of almighty God. Whatever the format of the service, hearts are lifted in true worship, and God is exalted.

A PLACE WHERE SPIRITUAL GIFTS ABOUND

The church of the future must release *all* the gifts of the Spirit. This generation wants spiritual ministry. The sick will be prayed for and the demonized delivered.

A PLACE WHERE SPIRITUAL BATTLES ARE WON

The church of the future must be an armory for spiritual soldiers. We must equip all of God's people with the sword of the Spirit and with prayer.

A PLACE WHERE THE HURTING ARE SHELTERED

One of the most hurtful and most difficult problems we are encountering is that of the abused woman. In our own ministry, we have reached out to help many women who have experienced spousal abuse. I feel some of the most devastating abuse is the sexual abuse of young girls by religious parents or family members. Sometimes very legalistic, strict parents are the worst victimizers.

Some time ago, I received a message from a very hurt woman who proceeded to complain about our ministry. Then she revealed that her preacher daddy visited her bedroom often until she ran away from home at age sixteen. Though she had become quite successful in life, she still blamed God for her past, and she harbored resentment toward all Christian leaders.

At a pastors' conference in another state, I was ministering at the close of a session when an astounding thing happened. I felt impressed to open the altar to minister to women who had been physically or sexually abused in the past. Immediately, the altar was crowded as twenty-three pastors' wives came forward, weeping. Most were under thirty-five years of age. As we ministered freedom and deliverance, most were overcome by the power of the Holy Spirit. God began closing emotional wounds and healing hearts that night.

A PLACE WHERE HEALING OCCURS

Many today would challenge the idea that God still heals people who are sick. However, the God who does not change still calls to the diseased and hurting soul, "I am the God that healeth thee!"

I have seen God's miraculous power firsthand, not only in my church but in my life and the lives of my family members. Several years ago while we were attending a convention meeting, my wife was very ill. She had been suffering from the effects of toxic shock syndrome and was almost too weak to stand, but she insisted on accompanying me to a Gaither concert held in the evening. As an introduction to the next song on the program entitled "It Is Finished," Gloria Gaither began calling out names of those for whom she sensed God was preparing a miracle. She declared, "Mrs. Phillips, it is finished tonight, and you are healed!"

Mrs. Gaither had not met us and did not know anything about Paulette. But as they sang that triumphant song, my wife was instantly healed!

A church that wants to minister in the fullness of the Holy Spirit will follow the biblical mandate to pray for the sick, anoint them with oil, lay hands upon them, and trust God in faith for healing. James admonished us, "Confess your trespasses to one another, and pray for one another, that you may be healed. The effective, fervent prayer of a righteous man avails much" (James 5:16 NKJV). This verse clearly advises us to first take care of our sin problems and then believe God for healing.

A PLACE WHERE FAMILIES ARE SAFE

The church must become family friendly. Children must be welcomed again into the life of the church. Church schedules must be simplified to give people time to be at home. Church events should promote family participation.

A PLACE WHERE THE BIBLE IS RELEASED IN THE LIVES OF THE PEOPLE

Many evangelical churches have raised a generation whose notebooks are full but whose hearts are cold. They may have all the answers, but possess no passion for ministry. They have sound theology, but no doxology. They can quote entire sermon outlines, but cannot get a word from God. The Jesus they know is trapped in their Bibles, notes, theology, and tradition. The living Christ is often missing in the zeal for religion.

The living Jesus wants to take His Word and use it to help others. Let us preach the good news, drive out devils, heal the sick, and see His kingdom on earth grow.

RECLAIMING WHAT IS YOURS

Out of a desperate hunger and need in my spirit, God brought me to a new level of spiritual life, and then poured out His renewal on my family and church. I continue to cherish the great doctrinal heritage that is mine, but I joyfully and fully embrace the move of God's Spirit.

My great hope is that evangelicals will discover the great variety of opportunity and experience that God has available for them. I don't feel every Christian has to have the same experiences as I did; however, I believe these experiences are valid both biblically and historically.

It is not a new thing—God's gifts have always been there for the claiming. Reach out and experience the abundant life of Holy Spirit fullness. You will never be the same.

NOTES

Preface

1. Henry Blackaby and Claude V. King, *Experiencing God* (Nashville: Broadman and Holman, 1998).

CHAPTER 1—A Journey Out of Death

1. Jack Taylor, *The Key to Triumphant Living* (Nashville: The Seedsowers, 1997).

CHAPTER 2—The Baptism of the Holy Spirit

1. R. A. Torrey, *The Holy Spirit: Who He Is and What He Does* (Old Tappan, NJ: Revell), 107–8.

2. As told in a sermon by R. A. Torrey, "Why God Used D. L. Moody," circa 1923, at Internet site http://www.revivalnet.com.

CHAPTER 3—A New Wineskin Church

1. Statistics from Brownsville revival Web site http://www.brownsville-revival.org.

CHAPTER 4—Untangling Tongues

1. Billy Graham, *The Holy Spirit* (Dallas: Word, 1988), 226, 234.

2. Michael Green, *I Believe in the Holy Spirit* (London: Hodder and Stoughton, 1975), 250.

3. Gordon Fee, *God's Empowering Presence: The Holy Spirit in the Letters of Paul* (Peabody, MA: Hendrickson Pub., 1994).

CHAPTER 5—Is the God of Miracles Still Present?

1. Jon Mark Ruthven, "Can a Charismatic Theology Be Biblical?" (Ph.D. diss., Regent University School of Divinity), 4, used by permission.

2. John MacArthur, *Charismatic Chaos* (Grand Rapids: Zondervan, 1992).

3. Jerry Vines, *Spirit Life* (Nashville: Broadman and Holman, 1998).

4. Jack Deere, *Surprised by the Power of the Spirit* (Grand Rapids: Zondervan, 1993).

5. Benjamin B. Warfield, *Counterfeit Miracles* (Edinburgh: Banner of Truth, 1992).

6. Dr. Lester Sumrall tells Dr. Bosworth's story in the book *Pioneers of Faith* (Tulsa: Harrison House, 1995).

CHAPTER 7—Was Paul a Charismatic?

1. James S. Stewart, *A Man in Christ: The Vital Elements of St. Paul's Religion* (New York: Harper and Row), 150, 154.

2. Ibid., discussed on 119–22.

3. Graham, *The Holy Spirit,* 225.

CHAPTER 9—Baptists and Other Heretics

1. Henry C. Vedder, *Short History of the Baptists* (Valley Forge, PA: Judson Press, 1967), 3–10.

2. Ibid., 9–10.

3. Thomas Armitage, *A History of the Baptists,* vol. 1 (New York: 1887).

4. Vedder, *Short History,* 119–25.

5. W. A. Jarrell, *Baptist Church Perpetuity* (Fulton, KY: National Baptist Publishing House, 1904), 69.

6. Ibid.

7. Ibid., 72.

8. Ibid., 73, citing Möller from *Schaff Herzog Encyclopedia,* vol. 2, 1562.

9. Ibid., citing Neander from *History of the Christian Church,* vol. 1, 518–19.

10. Ibid., 74, citing Thomas Armitage from *History of the Baptists,* 175.

11. Ibid., 75, citing William R. Williams from *Lectures on Baptist History,* 129, italics in original.

12. Ibid., 76, citing Möller from *Schaff Herzog Encyclopedia,* vol. 2, 1562, italics in original.

13. As told in Vedder, *Short History,* 137–56.

14. Ben M. Bogard, *Pillars of Orthodoxy, or Defenders of the Faith* (Fulton, KY: National Baptist Publishing House, 1901), 436.

15. John A. Broadus, *Sermons and Addresses* (Baltimore: R. H. Woodward, 1890), 228–30.

16. Frank Bartleman, *Another Wave of Revival* (Springdale, PA: Whitaker House, 1982), 26.

CHAPTER 10—Untidy Awakenings

1. John Wesley's Journal, May 21, 1740, in *The Journal of the Rev. John Wesley, A.M.,* vol. 2, ed. Nehemiah Curnock (London: Charles H. Kelly, 1909–16), 231–40.

2. Wesley, Journal, 151.

3. As told in Gerald McDermott, *Seeing God: Twelve Reliable Signs of True Spirituality* (Downers Grove, IL: InterVarsity, 1995).

4. John E. Smith, "The Distinguishing Marks of a Work of the Spirit," in the *Works of Jonathan Edwards,* vol. 4, *The Great Awakening* (New Haven and London: Yale University Press, 1972), 273.

5. Jonathan Edwards, "An Account of the Revival of Religion in North Hampton in 1740–42, as Communicated in a Letter to a Minister of Boston," in *Jonathan Edwards on Revival* (Carlisle, PA: Banner of Truth Trust, 1984), 150.

6. Winkie Pratney, *Revival* (Lafayette: Huntington House, 1994), 104, 26.

7. O. W. Taylor, *Early Tennessee Baptists* (Nashville: Tennessee Baptist Convention, 1957), 149–174.

8. Whitney R. Cross, *The Burned Over District: The Social and Intellectual History of Enthusiastic Religion in Western New York, 1800–1850* (New York: Harper and Row, 1950).

9. Helen Wessel, ed., *The Autobiography of Charles G. Finney* (Minneapolis: Bethany House, 1977), 100–101.

10. W. P. Strickland, ed., *Autobiography of Peter Cartwright: The Backwoods Preacher* (Ayer Co. Pub., 1856), 43.

11. Ibid., 45.

12. Ibid., 94.

CHAPTER 11—Moved by the Spirit of God

1. D. Martyn Lloyd-Jones, *God's Ultimate Purpose: An Exposition of Ephesians 1:1 to 2:3* (Grand Rapids: Baker Book House, 1978).

2. John Rogers, ed., *The Biography of Elder Barton Warren Stone, Written by Himself: With Additions and Reflections* (Cincinnati: J. A. and V. P. James, 1847; reprint, New York: Arno Press, 1972), 40–41.

3. Jonathan Edwards, *Religious Affections* (Edinburgh: Banner of Truth Trust, 1986).

4. Whitefield cited in Lloyd-Jones, *God's Ultimate Purpose*, 277–78.

5. Rogers, *Biography of Elder Barton W. Stone*, 41.

CHAPTER 13—Storming the Gates of Hell

1. Hymn by George Duffield Jr., "Stand Up, Stand Up for Jesus."

CHAPTER 14—He Makes Me Lie Down

1. Testimony of Paulette Phillips, used by permission.

2. Jonathan Edwards, "An Account of the Revival of Religion in North Hampton in 1740–42," 150.

3. Charles G. Finney, *Memoirs* (New York: A. S. Barnes and Co., 1876), 103.

CHAPTER 15—Quench Not the Spirit

1. Testimony of Heather Phillips Wooten, used by permission.

CHAPTER 16—Rivers of Living Water

1. *A River Runs Through It*, directed by Robert Redford, released 1992, by Filmayer S.A.

CHAPTER 17—The Church of the Future

1. Neil Anderson, *The Bondage Breaker* (Eugene, OR: Harvest House, 1990).

BIBLIOGRAPHY

Anderson, Neil T. *Victory Over the Darkness*. Ventura, CA: Regal Books, 1990.

Anderson, Neil T. and Elmer L. Towns. *Rivers of Revival*. Ventura, CA: Regal Books, 1997.

Baker, John. *Baptized in One Spirit*. Plainfield, NJ: Logos Books, 1967.

Bevere, John. *Breaking Intimidation: How to Overcome Fear and Release the Gifts of God in Your Life*. Lake Mary, FL: Creation House, 1995.

Brown, Michael L. *Let No One Deceive You: Confronting the Critics of Revival*. Shippensburg, PA: Revival Press, 1997.

Campbell, Wesley. *Welcoming a Visitation of the Holy Spirit*. Orlando, FL: Creation House, 1996.

Carrin, Charles. *Sunrise of David, Sunset of Saul*. Boynton Beach, FL: Charles Carrin Ministries, 1998.

Carroll, J. M. *The Trail of Blood*. Lexington, KY: Ashland Avenue Baptist Church, 1931.

Christenson, Larry. *Speaking in Tongues and Its Significance for the Church*. Minneapolis: Dimension Books, 1968.

Cymbala, Jim. *Fresh Wind, Fresh Fire*. Grand Rapids: Zondervan, 1997.

Frodsham, Stanley Howard. *Smith Wigglesworth: Apostle of Faith*. Springfield, MO: Gospel Publishing House, 1997.

Gilbert, Larry. *How to Find Meaning and Fulfillment Through Understanding the Spiritual Gift Within You*. Lynchburg, VA: Church Growth Institute, 1987.

Grudem, Wayne A. *Are Miraculous Gifts for Today?* Grand Rapids: Zondervan, 1996.

Jones, R. B. *Rent Heavens: The Welsh Revival of 1904*. Asheville, NC: Revival Literature.

Kydd, Ronald A. N. *Charismatic Gifts in the Early Church*. Peabody, MA: Hendrickson Pub., 1984.

—. *Healing Through the Centuries: Models for Understanding.* Peabody, MA: Hendrickson Pub., 1998.

Olford, Stephen F. *The Way of Holiness.* Wheaton, IL: Crossway Books, 1998.

Pierson, A. T. *The Acts of the Holy Spirit.* Harrisburg, PA: Christian Publications, 1980.

Potter, C. Burtt, Jr. *Baptists: The Passionate People.* Nashville: Broadman, 1973.

Rice, John R. *The Power of Pentecost or The Fullness of the Spirit.* Wheaton, IL: Sword of the Lord Publishers, 1949.

Riss, Richard and Kathryn. *Images of Revival: Another Wave Rolls In.* Shippensburg, PA: Destiny Image Publishers, 1997.

Robertson, A. T. *Paul the Interpreter of Christ.* Nashville: Broadman, 1921.

Ruthven, Jon Mark. "Can a Charismatic Theology Be Biblical? Traditional Theology and Biblical Emphases."

—. "Jesus as Rabbi: A Mimesis Christology: The Charismatic Pattern of Discipleship in the New Testament."

—. "On the Cessation of the Charismata: The Protestant Polemic on Post-Biblical Miracles."

Smith, G. *The Tozer Pulpit: Ten Messages on the Holy Spirit.* Harrisburg, PA: Christian Publications, 1968.

Taylor, Jack R. *After the Spirit Comes.* Nashville: Broadman, 1974.

Torbet, Robert G. *A History of the Baptists.* Valley Forge, PA: Judson Press, 1965.

Tuttle, Robert G. Jr. *The Partakers.* Nashville: Abingdon Press, 1974.

Watkins, Mamie. *The Baptism in the Holy Spirit Made Plain.* Greensburg, PA: Manna Christian Outreach, 1975.

Wood, A. Skevington. *And with Fire: Messages on Revival.* Ft. Washington, PA: Christian Literature Crusade, 1958.

ABOUT THE AUTHOR

RON PHILLIPS, pastor of east Tennessee's largest Southern Baptist church, has become a voice for spiritual renewal and awakening. Dr. Phillips sees his ministry as a bridge between evangelicals and charismatics. It is his prayer to see these two mighty movements develop unity and accomplish much together as a spiritual force.